Bureaucratic Nirvana
Life in the Center of the Box

Gaining Peace, Enlightenment and Potential Funding in the Pentagon R&D Bureaucracy

Hugh Montgomery

Preface by R. James Woolsey
Foreword by VADM Albert J. Baciocco, Jr., USN (ret.)

Second Edition

© Copyright 2013 Potomac Institute for Policy Studies

All rights reserved.
No part of this book may be reproduced in any form by any electronic or mechanical means (including photocopying, recording, or information storage and retrieval) without permission in writing from the Potomac Institute for Policy Studies.

Cover Design: Patrick Worcester

Published, 2013 by the Potomac Institute Press
Potomac Institute for Policy Studies
901 N. Stuart Street, Suite 200, Arlington, VA 22203
To order documents or for additional information:
www.potomacinstitute.org
Telephone: 703.525.0770; Fax: 703.525.0299
Email: webmaster@potomacinstitute.org

Second edition: ISBN-13: 978-0-9852483-9-0 paperback

TABLE OF CONTENTS

PREFACE VI
FOREWORD VII
ACKNOWLEDGEMENTS X
INTRODUCTION 11
BUREAUCRACY 101 15
    THE PRESIDENT'S BUDGET 15
BUREAUCRACY 201 19
    TECHNOLOGY READINESS LEVELS (TRLs) 19
    SCIENCE AND TECHNOLOGY 21
    THE VALLEY OF DEATH 21
    DOD BUDGET ACTIVITIES (BAs) 22
        BA 1. Basic Research 23
        BA 2. Applied Research 25
        BA 3. Advanced Technology Development 27
        The "Ditch of Death" 29
        Higher Categories of RDT&E 30
        BA 4. Advanced Component Development and Prototypes ... 30
        BA 5. System Development and Demonstration 31
        BA 6. RDT&E Management Support 31
        BA 7. Operational System Development 32
    RDT&E IDIOMS AND TERMS OF CONFUSION 32
        Program Element Numbers (PEs) vs. Budget Activities (BAs) ... 33
        Technology Base, Science and Technology and R&D 34
        ATDs, ACTDs and JCTDs 35
        Non-Acquisition BA4 and BA5 Programs 36
    CONGRESS AND THE DOD S&T BUDGET 37
    STRUCTURAL ROADBLOCKS TO TECHNOLOGY TRANSITION 37
    THE IMPORTANCE OF SERVICE S&T EXECUTION DIFFERENCES 41
        Air Force S&T Execution 41
        Naval S&T Execution 41

BUREAUCRACY 301 44
    BASIC RESEARCH (BA1) CULTURE – ACADEMIA 44
    APPLIED RESEARCH (BA2) AND ADVANCED TECHNOLOGY
    DEVELOPMENT (BA3) CULTURE – FEDERAL LABORATORIES
    AND FEDERALLY FUNDED R&D CENTERS (FFRDCs) 46
    ENGINEERING DEVELOPMENT AND PRODUCTION CULTURE –
    PRIVATE INDUSTRY 50
    INNOVATION VERSUS TECHNOLOGY 50
    TECHNOLOGY TRANSITION: 1950s – 1990s 52
    PARADIGM CHANGE #1 52
    PARADIGM CHANGE # 2 54
    PARADIGM CHANGE # 3 60

BUREAUCRACY 401 66
   UNDERSTANDING THE FEDERAL SYSTEM 66
   THE FEDERAL CULTURE 66
      Political Appointees 66
      Military Officers 70
      Career Civilians 76
      Military and Civilian Rank Equivalencies 81

BUREAUCRACY 501 84
   EXECUTION YEAR 85
   BUDGET YEAR, FEBRUARY – SEPTEMBER 87
   BUDGET YEAR, DECEMBER AND JANUARY 88
   BUDGET YEAR, OCTOBER AND NOVEMBER 89
   POM YEAR, JULY – SEPTEMBER 90
   POM YEAR, MAY – JUNE 91
   POM YEAR, FEBRUARY – APRIL 91
   POM YEAR, DECEMBER – JANUARY 92
   POM YEAR, OCTOBER – NOVEMBER 93

BUREAUCRACY 601 94
   DECISION-MAKING IN THE BUREAUCRACY 94
   WORKING INSIDE THE BUREAUCRACY 99
   25 COMMANDMENTS FOR BUREAUCRATS WORKING
   ON THE INSIDE 100
   MARKETING TO THE BUREAUCRACY 127
   12 COMMANDMENTS – FOR MARKETING TO FEDERAL EXECUTIVES 127

FINAL THOUGHTS 143

APPENDIX A 145
   HISTORY OF THE DEPARTMENT OF NAVY (DON)
   WARFARE CENTER SYSTEM 145

LIST OF ABBREVIATIONS 152

REFERENCES 155

INDEX 157

ABOUT THE AUTHOR 164

Bureaucratic Nirvana
Life in the Center of the Box

Gaining Peace, Enlightenment and Potential Funding in the Pentagon R&D Bureaucracy

Second Edition

Hugh Montgomery

The opinions expressed in this book are those of the author, and do not necessarily reflect the position of the Department of the Navy or the Potomac Institute for Policy Studies

PREFACE

Hugh Montgomery has given us an invaluable, practical, wry, readable, and quite humorous road map to how the federal government buys stuff, and indeed how it functions overall.

Although much of its specific examples are focused on the Navy and Research and Development (R&D), the book's delightful discussions of the different cultures involved in the acquisition process and the varying sets of "commandments" – for both those inside government and those wishing to understand the bureaucracy from the outside – are universally applicable.

In the book as a whole, Montgomery has pulled off something that is both extremely difficult and quite useful to a broad range of readers. He has used recollections and lessons from his very successful career as a canvas upon which to illustrate how things really work. Along the way he reminds (some of us) and teaches (others) the things you truly need to know, on both a day-to-day level (remind me, which level of admiral is a GS 17 equivalent to?), and the big picture you have to keep in mind ("Satan and the Comptroller never sleep"). In doing so he makes dealing with the US Government understandable, and does so with humor and flair.

Those of us who have spent at least part of our lives in government (in my case, 12 years divided among six different federal jobs) may skim the basic introductory portion but will read most of this fine book with a wry smile and continuing chuckles of recognition – seasoned by lots of muttering along the lines of, "wish to hell I'd thought of that 20 years ago." Those who are just beginning either federal service or a career that brings them into contact with government in any of a range of relationships should be deeply grateful for all the mistakes they don't stumble into because of Montgomery's fine work.

R. James Woolsey
Former Director, Central Intelligence Agency (1993-1995)

FOREWORD

The following text serves as a remarkably entertaining and accurate guide, if not a roadmap, to success for those who are serving or who seek to serve within the Federal Research and Development (R&D) bureaucracy. While principally using Department of Defense (DOD) organizations as the source and setting for deriving the content, lessons, principles, and "rules of the road" set forth herein, this book constitutes a rather complete compendium of valuable experience, knowledge and "guidance" useful to the men and women directly or indirectly involved in the R&D enterprise, whether a newcomer or a long-serving and seasoned public servant.

Hugh Montgomery has chosen to characterize his work as a journey along a self-described "path to peace and enlightenment in the Pentagon R&D bureaucracy". This characterization, while lightly humorous, provides exceptionally clear insight to the realities of working within this most complex of systems. The wisdom gained from the journey as described in this text can assist in shaping one's individual understanding and performance within the system and, in time, serve to improve the effectiveness of the system itself. In traversing the DOD R&D Program, prior to entering into discussion of the elements of that program, Technology Readiness Levels (TRLs) are discussed. While the TRLs described may be a relatively new (or – depending on one's perspective – old) term, the challenges described were real in yesterday's DOD, are very real today, and will continue to be real tomorrow, no matter what the term *du jour* may be. A fundamental appreciation and understanding of managing through the TRL challenges is well-presented as a precursor to descriptive discussions of Budget Activities, categories of research, technology transition, and the challenges of execution.

The author continues the "journey" into a historical examination of still-evolving changes to the Federal R&D Innovation and Technology Transition paradigm, including effects of these changes on the supporting performing agencies and execution infrastructure.

The content of this portion of the book highlights several areas of change that heretofore have often been overlooked or forgotten, but which have had a telling impact, both positive and negative, on our national capabilities for innovation and technology insertion into military systems. Clearly implied are periods of federal government and DOD policy changes that have resulted in unintended consequences on the R&D enterprise, affecting the stability of the R&D workforce and infrastructure, and causing a bureaucratic loss of balance between long term research efforts and near-term, requirements-driven R&D goals. The negative effects of such well-intentioned policy changes are not quickly or easily overcome.

A clear and frank presentation of the composition and characteristics of the cultures embedded in the federal R&D bureaucracy, and their strengths and weaknesses, provides accurate, valuable insight into understanding this essential component of R&D. While some of the characteristics cited may seem a bit harsh and worthy of further debate, elements of the profiles are reasonably discussed and objectively and fairly presented.

The "journey" continues with an obligatory (and valuable) description and discussion of the DOD R&D program and budget development process – somewhat of a primer, but an understandable presentation of a sometimes seemingly-arcane process. The information, presented using the Department of the Navy (DON) as the example, is succinct but complete. Embedded therein is sound guidance for any "outsider" seeking to interact with that process.

The "journey" is completed (for now) with a vigorous discussion of the "Inner Workings and Fundamental Truths of the Bureaucracy", and is generously laced with the author's admittedly personal opinions, anecdotes, half-truths and lies. The author provides – and discusses in some detail – his "25 Commandments for Bureaucrats working on the Inside". They may be humorous, *but they are sound!* They constitute experienced guidance based on the author's observations over a successful career traversing a rocky and challenging path. Clearly, worth paying attention to!

Montgomery accurately notes that "...except for those who have worked in senior headquarters assignment, most personnel inside the federal system are no better informed about how the system works that anyone else on the outside." He then offers "the following rules for development and marketing of a program for all, public or private sector, that compete for federal funding." He completes the "journey" with frank and thorough discussion on marketing to the bureaucracy, providing "12 Commandments for Marketing to Federal Executives". While these commandments are not carved into stone tablets, they do provide a concise listing of do's and don'ts. They are followed by a clear discussion of each, with examples and advice. Happily, one even includes a set of specific recommendations for a half hour (10-12 slides) Senior Executive briefing – a talent not solidly embedded or practiced within the bureaucracy today!

Of course, this "journey" will never be fully completed, but Hugh Montgomery has provided an interesting and comprehensive roadmap for successful travel within the challenging and complex Federal R&D bureaucracy. Understanding and practicing the principles outlined in this book can contribute to improving a process that is so vital to assuring our nation's military and economic future in a complex world.

Albert J. Baciocco, Jr.

Vice Admiral, U.S. Navy (Retired)
Former Chief of Naval Research (1978-1981)
Former Director Research Development and Acquisition – OP 098 (1983-1987)
Senior Fellow and Regent, Potomac Institute for Policy Studies

ACKNOWLEDGEMENTS

This work would not be complete without a sincere thank you to my friends and authors of the preface and foreword Jim Woolsey and Al Baciocco, who represent the best examples of how competent political appointees and senior military officers enrich the bureaucratic mix. Special thanks to Don Gay and Adam Nave who researched the budget information and developed the associated graphics, and to Fred Saalfeld and Tad Mackie, who provided welcome constructive criticism. Finally, neither the book nor the four decade career would have been possible without the love and support of my wife and only love Mitzie, and daughters Mindy and Michelle, who themselves have become successful senior public servants in the defense and justice departments.

INTRODUCTION

George Washington and Thomas Jefferson: fathers of the... bureaucracy? While we do not think of these revered Americans as designers of the system we love to hate, creation of an effective bureaucracy was, in fact, high on their list of lasting accomplishments. Driven by an overwhelming desire to ensure that America would never again be subject to the rule of a king, the founding fathers established the fundamental concept of separation of powers: three branches of government, each with equal powers and different (sometimes opposing) interests, and all having to reach a common consensus for the business of government to be conducted. The resulting structure was the first federal bureaucracy.

Despite numerous personal anecdotes and assertions to the contrary, the federal bureaucracy is logical, predictable and fiercely neutral. A complex collection of multiple players and moving parts, the "system" is nonetheless highly ordered and can be mastered by a skilled bureaucrat. Bureaucrats with the most prodigious skills tend to have low external profiles, thus may be invisible to the outside world – but there are many, and they make the system work.

In the 1930s, the German dictator and arguably the most evil leader of the 20th century proclaimed to devoted, but very misguided followers: "We are barbarians; it is an honorable title!" After spending more than four decades in and around the federal system, this writer found himself many times wanting to exclaim to the outside world: "We are bureaucrats; it is an honorable title!" It is the intent of this book to bring honor to the title "career bureaucrat" and to the kinder and gentler title "public servant," by shedding light on the inner workings of the federal system and its people. The federal government on the inside is a world that few have seen from other than a narrow perspective and, despite the system's inherent logic and predictability, even fewer understand or trust.

The focus of this book is on how the federal, and particularly the Department of Defense (DOD) and Research and Development (R&D) system operates on the inside; how and why decisions are made, and how outsiders can interact with the usually pretty smart people who make them. In this context, the term "decision-maker" refers to an individual with the ability to directly affect funding or major policy decisions for programs prior to their execution. While there are exceptions, this normally translates to a program size of at least many millions, and often billions of dollars, and a military rank of at the very least O-6 (Army, Air Force, or Marine Corps Colonel, or Navy Captain, or a corresponding civilian rank of GS-15), and usually higher.

Although most of my experience (thus my bias) is related to R&D in the Department of the Navy (DON) and DOD, the lessons learned apply to other federal and state bureaucracies, as well as to many private sector bureaucracies. Also, in terms of R&D level of effort, any unbiased investigation of federal funding will point immediately to DOD as the overwhelmingly largest player. DOD is not only the 800 pound gorilla in the room, but in terms of total R&D dollars, practically the only gorilla on the block. This is true in part because the US national security strategy assumes a requirement for a relatively small, but technologically superior military, ensuring that DOD is where the money is and, more often than not, where the most advanced technologies begin. It is difficult to compile a list of today's best known technologies (GPS, radar, laser, jet propulsion, microwave oven, digital computer, internet ...), that did not receive their first dollar from a DOD R&D program, even though they may have evolved or been perfected in the commercial world.

The book is written in the form of a "how-to" manual for people working inside the federal bureaucracy and also for those on the outside who receive (or desire to receive) federal dollars. Each of its six primary sections is designed to be relatively self-contained. As such, a small amount of redundancy is intentional and unavoidable. In many cases, the material is presented first in bulletized form, as a "pocket guide," followed by discussion of the same topic in greater detail. Those new to the federal bureaucracy will want to begin with the first chapter to develop a basic understanding of the President's Budget (PRESBUD), within the constraints of which the system operates. Those more familiar with the federal system may choose to begin reading at a later point.

Every bureaucracy even remotely worth its salt thrives on an internal vocabulary of highly specialized jargon, and federal acronyms will be used profusely in the pages that follow, although not without definition at least in their initial use. If, as a reader, you find this practice disturbing, my strong recommendation is that you put the book away immediately, do not reopen it, and either task your staff or hire a consultant to guide you through the intricacies and pitfalls of the federal system. You and the bureaucracy are highly unlikely to become good friends.

"The path to peace and enlightenment in the Pentagon R&D bureaucracy" is traversed in six primary sections:

Bureaucracy 101- **The President's Budget.** A brief overview of the Fiscal Year 2013 PRESBUD, with focus upon the Federal Agency R&D Budgets.

Bureaucracy 201- **The DOD RDT&E Program.** A discussion of the DOD Research, Development, Test and Evaluation funding categories and TRLs.

Bureaucracy 301- **The Changing R&D Innovation and Technology Transition Paradigm.** An analysis of the fundamental changes that have taken place in the national technology base over the past two decades and their impact on US technological leadership.

Bureaucracy 401- **The People of the Bureaucracy.** The three distinct cultures that make up the DOD system: political appointees, military officers and career civilians.

Bureaucracy 501- **DOD R&D Program and Budget Development.** How a federal budget is developed, and why the Congressional appropriation process necessitates very long term planning to begin new initiatives.

Bureaucracy 601- **The Inner Workings of the Federal R&D System.** How to not only survive, but to thrive in the federal system (Ph.D. level stuff – including personal anecdotes, opinions, half-truths and lies).

The Bureaucracy 102 and 102 chapters are presented in a broad overview style. More detailed information generally is available in various easy-to-locate government publications and websites. In latter chapters, a significant portion of the information is based entirely upon personal observations, and additional detail is provided. In most cases, names have been changed or omitted to protect the innocent and/or guilty. (Note: In a bureaucracy, determination of innocence or guilt may depend only on who is answering the question.) The author's understanding of the system evolved with experience and over many years, and a number of personal anecdotes and opinions (many quite strong) are included. Hopefully, the lines between fact and opinion have been drawn clearly for the reader.

The information presented requires an extremely significant caveat. The cultures and actions discussed represent the "normal" tendencies of the "average" political appointee, military officer or career civilian. There are numerous exceptions, *and it is precisely those exceptions that represent the best and the worst of the federal (or any bureaucratic) system.* The least competent executives can create enormous long-term damage; the most capable ones engage and innovate to keep the system afloat through the worst of natural and man-made emergencies. It is to those excellent, oft-maligned and almost universally underappreciated career senior bureaucrats that this book is dedicated.

BUREAUCRACY 101

The President's Budget

"Follow the money" is a phrase heard frequently in both public and private sector discussions. One of the most fundamental expressions of true priority is how an individual's – or a nation's – money is invested. In the case of the federal government, that priority is made public every January with the State of the Union Address and the accompanying release of the President's Budget Request (PBR or PRESBUD to appropriately initiated insiders). At the time of this writing, Congress is acting on the PRESBUD for Fiscal Year 2013 (FY-13), a total of almost four trillion dollars! Although the FY-13 budget will be used as the baseline for most of the discussions that follow, the spending percentages between agencies and categories historically tend to change only slightly from one year to the next. Despite a myriad of promises to the contrary every election year, the simple fact is that the majority of federal costs are fixed for many years into the future. Like starting, stopping or turning a supertanker, changing direction within the constraints of a congressionally appropriated federal budget – which also happens to carry the force of law – takes large amounts of time and space.

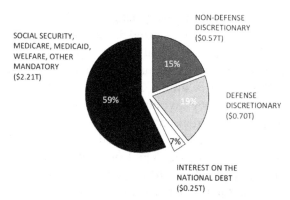

Figure 1. Fiscal Year 2013 President's Budget

Figure 1 presents a pie chart of the Fiscal Year 2013 President's Budget Request. A cursory inspection reveals that mandatory spending and interest on the debt make up two-thirds of the entire federal budget. Mandatory spending is growing rapidly – a very unhealthy budget situation, as it represents entitlement program spending, for which no direct service is performed for the taxpayer (Social Security, Medicare, Medicaid, federal retirement pensions, etc). Discretionary spending, on the other hand, includes the operating expenses of the federal agencies. The term "discretionary" is highly misleading, as specific commitments exist for most of the dollars long before they are appropriated by Congress or spent by federal agencies. Although the DOD share of the federal budget has declined steadily for decades, the Defense Budget remains the largest single component of federal discretionary expenses. The Defense Budget, however, is dwarfed by the rapidly-increasing magnitude of entitlement spending.

When the Research and Development (R&D) components of the 2013 President's Budget Request (Figure 2) are examined, DOD emerges as the overwhelming "big dog on the block." DOD investment represents slightly more than half of the national R&D base. The next largest investment area (Health Agencies) represents 22 percent of the total. The Department of Energy and NASA are next at 8 and 7 percent, respectively, and the other agencies share the remaining 12 percent of the federal R&D budget.

It comes as a great surprise to many people – and as a great disappointment to the plethora of Homeland Security-centric companies that appeared soon after 9/11 – that the Department of Homeland Security (DHS) executes such a small portion of the federal R&D investment. The reason is simple. As will be discussed in more detail later, federal agency investment levels are fixed for many years in advance, i.e., there is no new money. Thus the initial Department of Homeland Security R&D budget had to be derived from the combined existing R&D budgets of the 22 agencies that merged in 2002 to create DHS. Absent a sister federal agency offering to contribute funds to DHS' cause, the Agency's R&D bud-

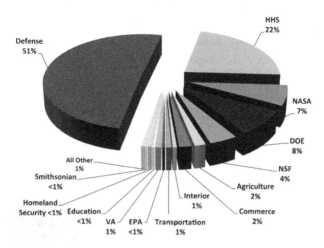

Figure 2. Fiscal Year 2013 Federal R&D President's Budget Request

get growth options were limited to: (1) zero-sum readjustments of the internal DHS budget pie (more dollars to R&D, offset by fewer dollars to other DHS programs); or (2) Congressional support for a larger pie (more dollars to DHS, offset by fewer dollars to all other federal agencies).

Though not the subject of this book, any objective discussion of the federal budget would be incomplete without pointing out that mandatory costs – *in the published President's Budget of record* – completely overwhelm federal discretionary spending in all categories in the immediate future – and the situation is rapidly growing worse! With projected annual federal deficit levels well in excess of 40% for 2013 and beyond, even cancellation of 100% of federal discretionary spending, *i.e., closing down all federal agencies, including Defense,* will not come close to balancing the budget! Current and future administrations and legislators face a Herculean task in controlling mandatory spending and balancing the federal budget while there is still time to do so – but time is very short. Figure 3, which uses the Administration's own budget projections for the next decade, depicts the growth in mandatory spending from the 2013 budget baseline. The impact of the stimulus spending, added to the exponential growth of entitlement programs, is readily apparent. Unfortunately, every increase in deficit spending exacerbates the problem.

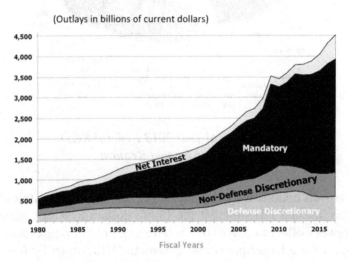

Figure 3. Projected Mandatory and Discretionary Federal Spending in the 2013 President's Budget

BUREAUCRACY 201
THE DOD RDT&E PROGRAM

Technology Readiness Levels (TRLs)

The first level of enlightenment in the world of DOD Research, Development, Test and Evaluation (RDT&E) Programs begins with an explanation of TRLs. The TRL concept was created by NASA and has been incorporated into the DOD lexicon within the last decade. TRLs have proven to be one of the most useful bureaucratic constructs, describing in a single number (from one to nine) the maturity and inherent technical risk of a technology or program. The Readiness Level concept is expanding and beginning to appear in other circles, e.g., Business Readiness Levels (BRLs), Manufacturing Readiness Levels (MRLs), etc. TRL definitions can be found at multiple locations on the web. The definitions listed in the table on the following page are available on the DOD Joint Capability Technology Demonstration website, http://www.acq.osd.mil/jctd/TRL.html[1] (re-printed here with permission).

Technology Readiness Level	Description
1. Basic principles observed and reported.	Lowest level of technology readiness. Scientific research begins to be translated into applied R&D. Examples might include paper studies of a technology's basic properties.
2. Technology concept and/or application formulated.	Invention begins. Once basic principles are observed, practical applications can be invented. Applications are speculative and there may be no proof or detailed analysis to support the assumptions. Examples are limited to analytic studies.
3. Analytical and experimental critical function and/or characteristic proof of concept.	Active R&D is initiated. This includes analytical studies and laboratory studies to physically validate analytical predictions of separate elements of the technology. Examples include components that are not yet integrated or representative.
4. Component and/or breadboard validation in laboratory environment.	Basic technological components are integrated to establish that they will work together. This is relatively "low fidelity" compared to the eventual system. Examples include integration of "ad hoc" hardware in the laboratory.
5. Component and/or breadboard validation in relevant environment.	Fidelity of breadboard technology increases significantly. The basic technological components are integrated with reasonably realistic supporting elements so it can be tested in a simulated environment. Examples include "high fidelity" laboratory integration of components.
6. System/subsystem model or prototype demonstration in a relevant environment.	Representative model or prototype system, which is well beyond that of TRL 5, is tested in a relevant environment. Represents a major step up in a technology's demonstrated readiness. Examples include testing a prototype in a high-fidelity laboratory environment or in simulated operational environment.
7. System prototype demonstration in an operational environment.	Prototype near, or at, planned operational system. Represents a major step up from TRL 6, requiring demonstration of an actual system prototype in an operational environment such as an aircraft, vehicle, or space. Examples include testing the prototype in a test bed aircraft.
8. Actual system completed and qualified through test and demonstration.	Technology has been proven to work in its final form and under expected conditions. In almost all cases, this TRL represents the end of true system development. Examples include developmental test and evaluation of the system in its intended weapon system to determine if it meets design specifications.
9. Actual system proven through successful mission operations.	Actual application of the technology in its final form and under mission conditions, such as those encountered in operational test and evaluation. Examples include using the system under operational mission conditions.

Science and Technology

A very important component of the RDT&E account is the set of programs of TRL 6 or below (Basic Research, Applied Research and Advanced Technology Development). These are known as Science and Technology (S&T) programs, indicating a relatively low level of technological maturity and a relatively high level of technological risk. S&T programs, by design, challenge and advance the state of the art, and thus are expected to have a significantly higher failure rate than the development efforts of acquisition programs – for which failure is not a viable option. The majority of DOD S&T programs and funds are managed by organizations with "Research" in their title, e.g., Defense Advanced Projects Research Agency (DARPA), Office of Naval Research (ONR), Air Force Office of Scientific Research (AFOSR) and Army Research Office (ARO). Their objective is the development – and transition – of science and technology. The process of discovery, however, is highly unpredictable and does not lend itself to precisely defined schedules. Their mission encourages innovation and rewards taking calculated risks.

The Valley of Death

The space between TRLs 6 and 7 is often referred to as the "Valley of Death," the space into which technologies frequently disappear, never to be seen again. The valley is created by an abrupt discontinuity in the cultures managing the programs, categories of funding and formal budget and program review process requirements. The relatively unstructured world of Science and Technology and non-acquisition dollars must be adapted to the formal and highly structured world of acquisition-specific development. The acquisition culture represents different people, in different organizations, with different objectives, operating in different chains of command. Even with all sides doing their best, crossing the valley can be very difficult.

TRL 7 ("demonstration of an actual system prototype in an operational environment") represents a major maturity step, and a crossover to the "Development" side of "Research and Development." At TRL 7, the technology or program is deemed to have sufficiently low risk as to allow its future cost and development schedule to be defined and included in the formal acquisition process. Programs of TRL 7 or greater are usually managed by "Systems Command" or "Materiel Command" type organizations, e.g., Army Materiel Command, Air Force Materiel Command, and Naval Air Systems Command. Their objective is to deliver effective systems within cost and schedule limitations to the warfighter.

Systems and Material Command missions and cultures are understandably risk-averse, and most of their program managers avoid even low-to-moderate risk-taking. The talented Colonels and Navy Captains who take risks and succeed in the execution of an important program, however, sometimes separate themselves sufficiently from their highly talented peer group to enable the difficult step upward, and to be selected for flag and general officer rank. On the other hand, taking risks and failing in a high-profile acquisition program is even more certain to result in instant (albeit negative) notoriety.

DOD Budget Activities (BAs)

The second level of enlightenment in the world of DOD RDT&E Programs begins with an understanding of the individual Budget Activities (BAs), ranging from BA1 Basic Research to BA7 Operational Systems Development. The taxonomy was created during the McNamara era of the 1960s, and is still used today. The separate budget categories will be discussed individually. The formal definitions and processes are documented in DOD Financial Management Regulation 7000.14-R – DOD Financial Management Regulation Volume 2B, Chapter 5 (Reference A)[2], and are also available on the web at www.defenselink.mil/ comptroller/regulations.html.

BA 1. Basic Research (6.1 Programs; TRLs 1-2)

BA 1 represents the front end of the long process from scientific discovery to fielded capability, generally associated with TRLs 1 and 2. According to Reference A, "Basic Research is systematic study directed toward greater knowledge or understanding of the fundamental aspects of phenomena and of observable facts without specific applications towards processes or products in mind. It includes all scientific study and experimentation directed toward increasing fundamental knowledge and understanding in those fields of the physical, engineering, environmental, and life sciences related to long-term national security needs. It is farsighted high payoff research that provides the basis for technological progress. Basic research may lead to: (a) subsequent applied research and advanced technology developments in Defense-related technologies, and (b) new and improved military functional capabilities in areas such as communications, detection, tracking, surveillance, propulsion, mobility, guidance and control, navigation, energy conversion, materials and structures, and personnel support. Program elements in this category involve pre-Milestone A efforts[3]."

"6.1 funding," as Basic Research is known to insiders, is (with a handful of notable exceptions) a long-standing preserve of the university community, which receives the great majority of the total BA 1 funding. The DOD FY-13 PRESBUD request was $2.1B, 3 percent of the RDT&E total. BA1 programs and funding tend to be relatively well-protected and thus highly stable for long periods.

Many people, especially within the university research community, are surprised to discover that DOD Basic Research spending in constant dollars has remained steady for decades, and is only slightly lower than levels during the Race to the Moon of the 1960s. BA1 tasks tend to be small, on the order of tens to hundreds of thousands of dollars, providing support for a university researcher and a small number of graduate students.

BA1 programs are managed through a fundamentally different process and culture than the other categories of RDT&E. They often represent long-standing relationships between researchers and sponsoring organizations and staff. Basic Research funding frequently is associated with specific individuals who may be renowned in their respective fields, and funding is frequently received in the form of research grants. The program review process of choice is peer review, and the product of a successful BA1 effort is publication in a respected peer-reviewed technical journal.

BA 2. Applied Research (6.2 Programs;TRLs 3-4, possibly TRL 5)

"Applied Research is systematic study to understand the means to meet a recognized and specific need. It is a systematic expansion and application of knowledge to develop useful materials, devices, and systems or methods. It may be oriented, ultimately, toward the design, development, and improvement of prototypes and new processes to meet general mission area requirements. Applied research may translate promising basic research into solutions for broadly defined military needs, short of system development. This type of effort may vary from systematic mission-directed research beyond that in Budget Activity 1 to sophisticated breadboard hardware, study, programming and planning efforts that establish the initial feasibility and practicality of proposed solutions to technological challenges. It includes studies, investigations, and non-system specific technology efforts. The dominant characteristic is that applied research is directed toward general military needs with a view toward developing and evaluating the feasibility and practicality of proposed solutions and determining their parameters. Applied Research precedes system specific technology investigations or development. Program control of the Applied Research program element is normally exercised by general level of effort. Program elements in this category involve pre-Milestone B efforts, also known as Concept and Technology Development phase tasks, such as concept exploration efforts and paper studies of alternative concepts for meeting a mission need (Reference A)[4]."

Applied Research – "6.2 funding" – may appear to an outside observer as a small technological maturity step from 6.1, but in reality it represents a step both across cultural boundaries, and from science to technology. The product of a Basic Research project is a publication, but the product of an Applied Research project is a proof-of-principle experiment or a "breadboard" system to demonstrate concept feasibility. A concept, however, may be a decade or more away from a fielded capability. BA2 tasks tend to be a few hundreds of thousands to ones of millions of dollars, enough to cover the labor costs of the task manager and sometimes a small staff, plus occasional breadboard-level fabrication.

While most Basic Research tasks are executed through universities, most Applied Research tasks are executed through federal laboratories, non-profit Federally Funded Research and Development Centers (FFRDCs, e.g., the Center for Naval Analyses) and University Affiliated Research Centers (UARCs, e.g., the Applied Research Laboratory at Penn State) and a few small companies that specifically focus on technology development. The timeline to application is far too long to entice the for-profit sector, especially large systems integrators, into investing significant manpower and funding resources in Applied Research.

Industry Independent Research and Development (IR&D)

It is important to realize that almost all large defense-related companies execute internal R&D programs known as Independent Research and Development (IR&D). Company leaders and their engineers will swear under oath that they conduct significant "research" under IR&D funding, and, from their perspective, this is true. Difficulty arises with the use of the term "research," which is very precise in federal budget terms and very imprecise almost everywhere else. This tends to add a great deal of confusion, especially for elected officials who desire to bring "research" dollars home to their districts. The character of the investment required for a non-profit research institution XYZ University and for a for-profit technology company XYZ Technologies, Inc. is very different, although it is not likely that either university officials or the company executives – and especially their elected representatives – would realize the significance of those differences.

This writer served as the first Navy IR&D Program Manager from 1981-1984 – during the peak of the Reagan Administration defense buildup. During those best of times for the military-industrial complex, with inflation-adjusted IR&D levels a factor of three or more higher than today's IR&D investment, the DOD's internal assessment indicated that only about 3.5 percent was *"Research"* in the TRL 1-4 context. Nearly 100 percent of industry's IR&D investment was then and is now focused on what DOD would classify as "Development," i.e., R&D efforts that are within a two year time window to profitability (TRL 7 and higher). This is a good news story rather than bad, and helps to ensure that government, industry and academia very rarely duplicate effort or compete unnecessarily with each other.

This confusion of terms, however, has a definite negative impact on the Basic and Applied Research balance in the Congressional appropriation process. Most Congressional districts include multiple colleges and universities, which become powerful indigenous lobbies for Basic Research funding. Applied Research, however, is executed largely by federal laboratories, and their employees are prohibited by law from lobbying. The legal prohibition is almost a moot point; members of the federal Science and Engineering culture usually represent the most inept of lobbyists. The result is that the Basic Research budget in constant dollars has been relatively stable since the Viet Nam era, while Applied Research investment has dropped dramatically. This will be discussed in greater detail in later chapters. The Applied Research request in the DOD FY-13 PRESBUD is $4.5B, representing 6.5 percent of the RDT&E total.

BA 3. Advanced Technology Development (6.3 Programs; TRLs 5-6)

Advanced Technology Development "includes development of subsystems and components and efforts to integrate subsystems and components into system prototypes for field experiments and/ or tests in a simulated environment. [BA 3] includes concept and technology demonstrations of components and subsystems or system models. The models may be form, fit and function prototypes or scaled models that serve the same demonstration purpose. The results of this type of effort are proof of technological feasibility and assessment of subsystem and component operability and producibility rather than the development of hardware for service use. Projects in this category have a direct relevance to identified military needs. Advanced Technology Development demonstrates the general military utility or cost reduction potential of technology when applied to different types of military equipment or techniques. Program elements in this category involve pre-Milestone B efforts, such as system concept demonstration, joint and Service-specific experiments or Technology Demonstrations and generally have TRLs of 4, 5, or 6. Projects in this category do not necessarily lead to subsequent development or procurement phases, but should have the goal of moving out of Science and Technology (S&T) and into the acquisition process within the future years defense program (FYDP). Upon successful completion of projects that have military utility, the technology should be available for transition (Reference A)[5]."

Advanced technology development denotes a degree of technological maturity that still includes a significant element of risk, but allows demonstration of the technology in a realistic environment. BA 3 projects tend to be two to five years away from production and profitability, but they are close enough to profit fruition to be seriously noticed by the private sector. BA 3 was created in 1977 under the name "6.3A," to connote a technology of sufficient maturity to be prototyped, but not sufficiently mature to become a baseline technology within an acquisition program. The product of a BA 3 program usually is a fieldable prototype, or "brassboard" system. The concept of "Advanced Technology

Demonstrations (ATDs)" was developed specifically to address the risk-reduction demonstrations necessary before technology is accepted in a planned system acquisition.

Although military Service ATDs and DOD Advanced Concept Technology Demonstrations (ACTDs) and Joint Capability Technology Demonstrations (JCTDs) are classic (and the most visible) examples of Advanced Technology Development programs, BA 3 also includes continuing long-term level-of-effort programs for technologies that need additional risk reduction and maturity before being transitioned into an acquisition program.

The BA 3 DOD FY-13 PRESBUD request is $5.3B, 7.6 percent of the RDT&E total (Overall, the S&T account represents 17 percent of the DOD RDT&E total.). BA3 tasks tend to range in size from ones to tens on millions of dollars, enough money to develop, fabricate and conduct a risk-reduction demonstration of a brassboard-level prototype system. At the conclusion of a successful demonstration, the acquisition community should feel a sufficient level of comfort that the program risk is acceptably low so as to allow insertion of the technology into a formal acquisition program – beyond TRL 6, and on the other side of the "Valley of Death."

BA 3 represents the last point at which a technology can afford to fail. My opinion and rule of thumb, based on more than four decades of experience, is that in an ideal program, about one-third of BA 3 programs should fail to transition (for all causes). A significantly higher failure rate indicates too much program risk (probably should have received BA 2 funding), and a significantly lower rate indicates little or no risk, in which case the program is not Science and Technology in character. Higher categories of development normally are associated with the DOD's formal acquisition process (and are not discussed in depth in this book), within which failure for technical reasons generally is not considered to be an option.

The infamous "Valley of Death" separates moderate and high risk S&T from the formal acquisition process. Separating the categories and cultures within the S&T community is a chasm that is less deep, but just as real, that I, half-seriously, refer to as the "Ditch of Death" – the crossover from science to technology.

The "Ditch of Death"

The typical scientist conducting Basic Research and early-stage Applied Research resides in an institution of higher learning, pursuing a goal of publication in a respected scientific journal, after a rigorous peer review process. Researchers are judged and rewarded according to the number and quality of successful publications. Costs tend to be driven by the labor costs of the researcher, frequently assisted by (relatively low cost) graduate students, as well as the costs of laboratory equipment and experimentation. Programs generally have long-term stability, take many years to come to fruition, and often have hard-to-predict schedules. This process is entirely appropriate for BA1 funding and absolutely necessary for the steady advancement of science and education.

The typical scientist or engineer conducting later-stage Applied Research or Advanced Technology Development (referred to from this point forward as "technologists," as opposed to "researchers") is more likely to be found in a federal or private sector laboratory pursuing a goal of technology transition, near-term to higher categories of development and far-term into production and implementation within a larger system. Technologists are less likely to take a "handoff" from an individual Basic Researcher than to apply the accumulated science from multiple Basic Research efforts. Technology development usually is conducted with specific applications in mind, and it is not uncommon for a technologist to remain attached to a project all the way through development and production, from so-called "cradle to grave".

Because of these cultural and value-set differences, technology development rarely follows a linear path from Basic Research to production. Instead path linearity begins across the "Ditch of Death" at BA 2, and sometimes BA 3. Individuals on each side of the ditch have great respect for one another, but their natural interests and biases tend to make everyday communication difficult. Both sides believe in their heart of hearts that they are working on the more challenging (and more important) end of the problem. Fortunately, for each side, they are!

Higher Categories of RDT&E

Transition of an S&T program into Budget Activities 4 and 5 (Development and Engineering) represent a crossover to the acquisition side of the "Valley of Death," entry into the in the formal acquisition process and culture and a major step toward turning technology into a fielded capability. Development and Engineering programs total $27.1B in the 2013 PRESBUD, 39 percent of the DOD RDT&E budget. Because successful navigation through the acquisition process leads to production and sales, these accounts are aggressively pursued by American industry. At this stage of development, risk issues are not so much technology-related as related to systems engineering and first-time integration of multiple technologies into systems.

BA 4. Advanced Component Development and Prototypes (ACD&P – 6.4 Programs)

According to Reference A, BA 4 consists of "efforts necessary to evaluate integrated technologies, representative modes or prototype systems in a high fidelity and realistic operating environment are funded in this budget activity. The ACD&P phase includes system specific efforts that help expedite technology transition from the laboratory to operational use. Emphasis is on proving component and subsystem maturity prior to integration in major and complex systems and may involve risk reduction initiatives. Program elements in this category involve efforts prior to Milestone B and are referred to as advanced component development activities and include technology demonstrations. Completion of TRLs 6 and 7 should be achieved for major programs. Program control is exercised at the program and project level. A logical progression of program phases and development and/or production funding must be evident in the FYDP [Future Year Development Plan][6]." ACD&P programs total $12.4B in the 2013 PRESBUD, 18 percent of the DOD RDT&E budget.

BA 5. System Development and Demonstration (SDD 6.5 Programs)

"SDD programs have passed Milestone B approval and are conducting engineering and manufacturing development tasks aimed at meeting validated requirements prior to full-rate production. This budget activity is characterized by major line item projects and program control is exercised by review of individual programs and projects. Prototype performance is near or at planned operational system levels. Characteristics of this budget activity involve mature system development, integration and demonstration to support Milestone C decisions, and conducting live fire test and evaluation (LFT&E) and initial operational test and evaluation (IOT&E) of production representative articles. A logical progression of program phases and development and production funding must be evident in the FYDP consistent with the Department's full funding policy[7]." System Development and Demonstration Programs total $14.7B in the 2013 PRESBUD, 21 percent of the DOD RDT&E budget.

BA 6. RDT&E Management Support (6.6 Programs)

As stated in Reference A, Budget Activity 6 "...includes research, development, test and evaluation efforts and funds to sustain and/or modernize the installations or operations required for general research, development, test and evaluation. Test ranges, military construction, maintenance support of laboratories, operation and maintenance of test aircraft and ships, and studies and analyses in support of the RDT&E program are funded in this budget activity. Costs of laboratory personnel, either in-house or contractor operated, would be assigned to appropriate projects or as a line item in the Basic Research, Applied Research, or Advanced Technology Development program areas, as appropriate. Military construction costs directly related to major development programs are included.[8] In short, BA 6 represents the "overhead" kinds of functions associated with R&D (e.g., the operating budget for the Office of Naval Research and the Center for Naval Analyses). BA 6 funding tends to be very stable, as increases or reductions have near-term impacts on manpower and infrastructure. The FY-13 PRESBUD request for BA 6 is $4.3B, 6 percent of the RDT&E total.

BA 7. Operational System Development (6.7 Programs)

"This budget activity includes development efforts to upgrade systems that have been fielded or have received approval for full rate production and anticipate production funding in the current or subsequent fiscal year. All items are major line item projects that appear as RDT&E Costs of Weapon System Elements in other programs. Program control is exercised by review of individual projects. Programs in this category involve systems that have received Milestone C approval. A logical progression of program phases and development and production funding must be evident in the FYDP, consistent with the Department's full funding policy (Reference A).[9]" For many years, BA 7 programs tended to go unnoticed within the system. However, as systems age and maintenance becomes more important, BA 7 dollars to fund the R&D necessary to keep the fielded systems in operation becomes more important. The 2013 PRESBUD request for BA 7 is $26.4B, 38 percent of the total DOD RDT&E investment.

RDT&E Idioms and Terms of Confusion

Every great language has its own unique terms (idioms) that make little or no sense when interpreted literally. Bureaucracies are no exception.

Program Element Numbers (PEs) vs. Budget Activities (BAs)

In 1977, DOD divided Budget Activity Three into non-acquisition (6.3A) and acquisition (6.3B) accounts. Although work in both categories was of the character of Advanced Development, the 6.3A programs were not part of a formal requirements-driven acquisition process, while 6.3B programs responded to formal requirements and were closely aligned to acquisition of systems. 6.3A programs were aligned for budget purposes with BA 1 and BA 2 (Technology Base) programs to create the category known today as Science and Technology (S&T). The bureaucratic construct of 6.3A and 6.3B programs created mild confusion, as the Program Element (PE) numbers gave no indication which was which. PEs for both categories began with the numbers 0603, and program managers referred to each – correctly – as "6.3 programs." The PE numbering system was otherwise fully consistent; 6.1 PEs began with the numbers 0601, 6.2 with 0602, 6.4 with 0604, etc.

Two decades later, DOD changed the Budget Activity numbering system in a way that only a comptroller could love. The change dramatically increased the confusion level and caused many both within and outside the system to shake their heads in disgust. Budget Activities for 6.1-6.3A programs remained in alignment, BAs 1, 2 and 3, respectively. The previous 6.3B category ACD&P became BA4 (6.4), and the numbering system for every higher category ratcheted up a notch, ending at BA7 (Operational System Development). So far, so good.

A disconnect was introduced, however, when the corresponding higher category Program Element numbers were not changed in parallel, i.e., BA4 PEs began with the numbers *0603xxx*, BA5 PEs began with numbers *0604xxx*, and so forth. Although precise application of the term "6.3 funding" refers specifically to a BA3 non-acquisition S&T program, in more common use the term "6.3 funding" is equally likely to refer to a BA4 acquisition program – for which the fourth digit of the Program Element number is 3. A personal recommendation to the DOD Comptroller, made in the 1990s and offered again today, is once and for all to align PE and

BA numbers so as to correspond directly to each other. Confusion will continue to exist so long as a one-digit transformation is required between the two for BAs 4-7.

Technology Base, Science and Technology and R&D

As previously discussed, prior to 1977, RDT&E programs considered to be technology-related were called Technology Base, consisting of Budget Activity 1 (Basic Research) and Budget Activity 2 (Applied Research, then known as Exploratory Development). In 1977 the Advanced Technology Development (BA3) account was created, and Science and Technology (S&T) became the term of choice for technology-related programs. This budget construct allowed the Secretary of Defense to proudly proclaim in 2006 that the R&D Budget of that year contained the largest Defense S&T investment in history. Technically, this statement is true, but it does not represent an accurate picture of the truth. That is because Technology Base (6.1 + 6.2) investments of the space-race days of the 1960s were far higher than today's total S&T investment. If we were to include in the 1960s totals the budgets for those programs that correspond to today's BA3 investments, it would make the differences even larger. Very few observers are aware of this important fact, and of the equally important reality that most technologies we enjoy today (e.g., GPS, lasers, integrated circuits, ball-point pens) were invented during a time of far more robust national technology base investment.

Today's Basic Research investment is lower, but still is relatively healthy as compared to the levels of the 1960s. On the other hand, investments in Applied Research, necessary to carry research to the next level and arguably the engine driving America's technological edge, has remained in steady decline from the late 1960s into the 21st century, and today remains dramatically lower than levels of the past. Other than a smaller number of scientists and engineers in relevant fields and institutions today, there is no way to assess the lost opportunity, or to determine the inventions that were never made because of these prior reductions to Applied Research in the US.

ATDs, ACTDs and JCTDs

In 1985, I was the creator of Advanced Technology Demonstrations (ATDs), designed as risk-reduction programs to prototype, demonstrate and transition the highest payoff emerging technologies. System risk is usually related to one or a small number of components. Thus, successful demonstration of those risky components may allow crossing of the "Valley of Death" in far shorter times and at far lower cost than for a full system demonstration.

ATDs were selected through a very rigorous process. Only 6-8 were approved from an initial number of over 100 proposals. Final approval required acquisition funding to be in place to ensure no chance of falling into the "Valley". Even though Naval ATDs represented higher than normal risk for the BA3 category, over two-thirds successfully transitioned into development, a far higher number than the lower-risk non-ATD part of the Naval BA3 investment. In 1988, the Defense Science Board (DSB) reviewed the Navy ATD Program and stated that ATDs were the "model DOD technology transition program," and recommended that "all Services dedicate at least 50 percent of the 6.3A investment" to ATDs.[10] Relevant sections of the 1985 Navy ATD Program Instruction[11] were used verbatim by the DSB in its report.

A problem arose, however, because of the unfortunate choice of title and acronym – ATD. The mistake is one for which I bear much of the responsibility. In 1985, as a new member of the Senior Executive Service, I was still naive with respect to (1) the importance of titles and (2) the cleverness of the career senior bureaucrats, who adhere to the practice of cultural pessimism – an appropriate religion in a bureaucracy – and for whom, as we shall discuss later, change is initially resisted, an appropriate initial response in a bureaucracy.

The title of the BA3 category is Advanced Technology Development, which of course, leads to the same acronym – ATD. The simple bureaucratic solution for full compliance with DSB and DOD guidance was to apply the ATD acronym in its broad sense, and voila, success is achieved overnight! As a result, few non-Navy programs called ATDs included any requirement for dedicated transition funding – the essential ingredient for transition success and a required component for 100 percent of Naval ATDs. Today's most advanced fire control algorithms, quiet propulsion systems, enclosed ship masts, explosive storage magazines and DNA-based vaccines were carried across the "Valley of Death" as ATDs.

In 1994, the Deputy Undersecretary of Defense (Advanced Systems and Concepts), created Advanced Concept Technology Demonstrations (ACTDs), known today as Joint Capability Technology Demonstrations (JCTDs). ACTDs extended the ATD concept into the arena of joint programs, in which the demonstrations and exercises investigated concepts of operations as well as technologies. Current systems such as the Predator and Global Hawk represent examples of ACTD successes.

Non-Acquisition BA4 and BA5 Programs

As a rule, programs funded in Budget Activities 4 and 5 are part of the formal DOD acquisition process (Reference B). There are, however, small pockets of funding BA 4/5 funding that supports projects which are of a maturity level beyond greater than TRL 6, but which do not directly lead to systems acquisition. Because they comprise a very small percentage of the BA 4/5 total, they tend to be ignored (at least for the most part). Because of the loose oversight of these dollars, they become for many the *de facto* contingency fund. While these words may make most CPAs blanche, such a system is by far preferable to the alternative of reprogramming from ongoing acquisition programs, which would produce a constant stream of schedule disruptions and cost increases.

Congress and the DOD S&T Budget

Anytime one wants to examine Congressional earmarks in detail, a good place to begin is in the DOD S&T budget. We have seen already that DOD has the largest R&D budget, which makes DOD is the easiest place for a member of Congress to add the most dollars with the least visibility. S&T also is the easiest place within DOD to add the most dollars with the least major program disruption.

An example: In FY-08, the Army requested a total of $1.73B for Science and Technology in the PRESBUD. The Congress appropriated a total of $2.89B, an increase of 67 percent above the request. A large part of the increase was for breast cancer research, for which Congress has added hundreds of millions of dollars to the Army S&T budget for a number of years. The official congressional rationale for breast cancer research in a military budget is not without merit. Members of the military provide a large control population of exceptionally physically fit subjects for study, subjects who can be tracked easily for many years into the future. The unofficial reason, however, is more practical and compelling. Among the federal agencies' R&D budgets, only within DOD can hundreds of millions of earmarked dollars be absorbed on an annual basis without high visibility. This is in no way a criticism of breast cancer research as worthy investment in public health – which it most certainly is. However, even staunch supporters of breast cancer research (a group in which I am included) would be hesitant to describe breast cancer as a critical warfighting issue.

Structural Roadblocks to Technology Transition

For anyone with even the most rudimentary understanding of Budget Activities, it becomes apparent that transition of technology programs across the "Valley of Death" is a far more straightforward process when an agency controls its own destiny (i.e., controls budget decisions for both S&T and acquisition dollars). This is illustrated clearly by Figure 4, which shows the DOD

Research and Engineering (S&T plus BA4) PRESBUD request. Each of the military Services has a robust BA4 program to provide dollars to "pull" technology across the "Valley" and into funded acquisition programs.

The Defense Advanced Projects Research Agency (DARPA), despite its large S&T funding total, does not control the ACD&P (BA4) funding necessary to carry its own work forward. This adds a significant complication for DARPA with respect to technology transition. No matter how worthwhile or revolutionary a new concept may be, DARPA must rely on the military services or other agencies to transition its work. Thus, for its technology initiatives to succeed, DARPA must develop its transition plans in concert with the budget requests of other federal entities. As we shall see later, this necessitates close coordination an absolute minimum of two years in advance (if not more – preferably three or four).

The two year minimum for federal budget insertion is driven by the Congressional process for appropriating dollars. Only a small fraction of the staff of any federal agency understands either the requirement for such advance planning or the reasons for its existence. Technology transition, which is at best a challenge even for services or agencies that control their own BA4 funding, becomes inherently (i.e., structurally) more difficult for those that must depend on other activities to carry their products forward into development and production.

An interesting special case of technology transition budgeting is illustrated in Figure 4 by the column labeled "MDA (Missile Defense Agency)," known in the 1990s as the Ballistic Missile Defense Office (BMDO) and in the 1980s as the Strategic Defense Initiative Office (SDIO, more popularly called "Star Wars"). The chart indicates very little S&T funding, but an unusually large BA4 budget – exactly the opposite of DARPA's funding balance. DARPA's budget, however, paints a more accurate transition picture than MDA's, which in reality is an artifact from an event that occurred in the early 1990s.

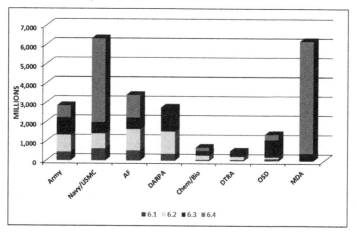

Figure 4. FY-13 DOD Research and Engineering (BA1- BA4) PRESBUD Request
Adapted and reprinted with permission from DDR&E

During a review of the FY 1994 DOD S&T budget by the Joint Requirements Oversight Council (JROC, chaired by the Vice Chairman of the joint Chiefs of Staff and including as members the Vice Chiefs of each of the Services), I presented a slide that illustrated the Services' S&T budgets in a constant-dollar decline and Defense Agency budgets in rapid constant-dollar growth. There was much discussion and concern expressed by the JROC members as to whether or not this represented the best DOD investment strategy. I was the final presenter of the day, to be followed when the meeting reconvened a week later by the BMDO (now MDA) representative. When that speaker presented the Defense Agency budget charts, the totals now showed sharp declines in FY 1995 and beyond – although the same program had been on a steep growth curve only a week earlier. In anticipation of difficult JROC questions on S&T budget growth, BMDO had reclassified most of their BA3 investment to BA4 during the intervening week. The previous steep growth of the BMDO S&T budget now showed a precipitous decline, while the BA4 acquisition budget appeared to be much healthier! The planned program of record, however, was precisely the same as before. Previous year budgets also were adjusted accordingly in the charts, in order to maintain "consistency."

This case is not intended as a criticism of BMDO. Budget category adjustment and perception management are tools used by successful federal and private sector entities alike to minimize vulnerability of programs, policies and dollars. Because the old saying "figures lie and liars figure" can be applied to virtually every large budget, it is important to understand the whole budget story, including the underlying assumptions, before conclusions are drawn. In the final accounting, organizations that are unable to adapt and to be creative when the need arises become the first to lose their funding.

The Importance of Service S&T Execution Differences

Each of the four military services handles its S&T dollars and infrastructure in a different way. The differences are significant, and important to understand in doing business with each service. The Air Force and the Navy represent the extremes of the system, with the Army and Marine Corps operating in between.

Air Force S&T Execution

The Air Force executes Science and Technology programs via a centralized structure, under the Air Force Materiel Command and the Air Force Research Laboratory (AFRL). Air Force S&T is characterized by a strong military presence, with young officers trained in science and engineering disciplines working alongside civilians with similar training. AFRL personnel are institutionally funded, meaning that salaries are paid up front from the BA 2 Applied Research account. The Air Force Applied Research budget appears on paper to be significantly larger than for the other services, but to make an apples-to-apples comparison, one must take into account the dollars dedicated to the AFRL manpower costs. More important to the private sector, the effect is that a $300K Red Widget program at AFRL provides for up to the full $300K to be made available for outside contracts in support of the Red Widget program execution. Much of the Air Force S&T program execution occurs through contractors, such that the private sector perceives AFRL to be a potential sponsor and a source of funding.

Naval S&T Execution

The Naval S&T Program features centralized funding and program management via the Office of Naval Research. Execution, however, is decentralized, and conducted via the Naval Research Laboratory (NRL, which reports to ONR), the Marine Corps Warfighting Laboratory (MCWL, reporting to the Marine Corps Combat Development Command) and four Naval Warfare Centers: the Naval Air Warfare Center (NAWC, reporting to the

Naval Air Systems Command), Naval Surface Warfare Center (NSWC, reporting to the Naval Sea Systems Command), Naval Undersea Warfare Center (NUWC, reporting also to the Naval Sea Systems Command) and SPAWAR Systems Center (SSC, reporting to the Space and Naval Warfare Systems Command). Naval Warfare Centers have multiple sites and divisions, each operating relatively independently, with a Navy Captain as Commanding Officer and a senior civilian as Technical Director. NSWC, for example, has major R&D divisions at Carderock and Indian Head, MD, Dahlgren, VA, Panama City, FL, Corona and Port Hueneme, CA and Crane, IN.

In the Navy system, military presence is much more limited than in the Air Force, and serves to command the activity and to ensure Naval relevance of the technical work. Almost all of the hands-on science and engineering is conducted by career civilians.

The Naval Research laboratory and all Naval Warfare Centers are industrially funded, meaning that the salaries of the scientists and engineers must be paid by project funds. The same hypothetical $300K Red Widget program discussed above, if executed at NRL or a Naval Warfare Center, might engage the first $250K to pay for in the in-house engineer, leaving only $50K for potential contract support. For this reason, private sector companies that view the Air Force as a potential sponsor may view the Navy as a potential competitor.

This characterization does not apply, however, to the Marine Corps Warfighting Laboratory (MCWL). MCWL receives its S&T funding via ONR, but otherwise operates in a manner closer to the Air Force model. With a strong military presence at all levels, including a Commanding General (who serves also as the Vice Chief of Naval Research), senior and junior officers and a Special Purpose Marine Air-Ground Task Force, MCWL issues contracts to both private and public sector activities for program execution. Like the Marine Corps model, the Army operates between the opposite poles of the Air Force and Navy, with program execution and policies that tend to be somewhat more site specific.

One very important fact applies to all service R&D laboratories; they have no budget authority other than to execute programs of record. With very few exceptions, they do not have delegated authority to initiate programs on their own; program policy and funding decisions are made at the service headquarters level. Field activities may have considerable latitude in the execution of their programs of record, but not in the creation of new ones.

For readers who may be interested in additional information on the DOD laboratories, I prepared a history of the Naval R&D Laboratory System as part of a previous study. It is included as Appendix A.

BUREAUCRACY 301
THE CHANGING R&D INNOVATION AND TECHNOLOGY TRANSITION PARADIGM

Since WWII, the US national security strategy has been based upon the assumption of technological superiority with respect to our adversaries. In the early days of the Reagan defense buildup, Secretary of Defense Caspar Weinberger wrote; "We face the danger of losing our edge because we have not adequately replenished the reservoir of scientific concepts and knowledge to nourish future technologies during subsequent years of fiscal neglect of defense R&D. Given these circumstances, we must systematically replenish that scientific reservoir, using the unique and diverse strengths of the United States scientific community ... Given the relatively long lead time between fundamental discovery and applying such knowledge to defense systems, the true measure of our success ... may not be apparent for several decades. When the 'moment of truth' arrives, we cannot afford to be found wanting. Thus we must revitalize the productive partnership between the university community, industry, and the DOD in-house laboratories."[12]

Since the end of the Reagan administration, the national paradigm for technology transition has undergone a very quiet, yet very significant transformation. This section examines those changes and their impact upon our national ability to achieve and maintain technical innovation and superiority. We shall begin with a discussion of the cultures that make up the American R&D establishment, their unique identities, and complementary roles. For those who may have skipped the discussion in the Bureaucracy 201 chapter, there is a small amount of deliberate overlap in this section.

Basic Research (BA1) Culture – Academia

In August 1944, President Franklin D. Roosevelt wrote to Dr. Vannevar Bush, Director of the Office of Scientific R&D[13], asking how the successful application of scientific knowledge to wartime problems could be carried over into peacetime. Dr. Bush responded in July 1945 with a seminal report to the President entitled "Science, the Endless Frontier[14]." In August 1946, less than a year after the end of the war, President Truman signed Public Law 77-588, establishing the Office of Naval Research (ONR) to plan, foster, and encourage scientific research as related to future naval power and national security. Four years later, he signed Public Law 81-507, establishing the National Science Foundation (NSF). ONR's first Director, Dr. Alan Waterman also served as the first Director of NSF. The creation of ONR, NSF, the Air Force Office of Scientific Research (AFOSR) and the Army Research Office (ARO) established a 50-year paradigm that stood for execution and transition of research and technology in the United States.

The vast majority of DOD Basic Research dollars are expended in universities. Within this culture, the overall focus is long term; scientific discovery that may bear fruit and lead to future capabilities in decades rather than in months or years. Program selection tends to occur on a far more personal level than for other categories of RDT&E. Research dollars flow to noted scientists, based upon their past successes in the field. In addition, there have been concentrated efforts to find outstanding young scientists and move them into the DOD sphere of influence. Because of these personal relationships and the evolutionary character of scientific research and experimentation, Basic Research programs tend to have long term objectives and budget stability. The product (and metric for success) of a Basic Research effort is publication in a respected peer-reviewed technical journal.

Figure 5 shows the DOD S&T Budget (FY-06 PRESBUD) in constant dollars. The choice of illustrating FY-06 is because that year represents the highest DOD S&T PRESBUD proposal in the post Viet Nam era. The BA1 line shows that, except for a drop in the mid-1970s, when universities tended to distance themselves from defense research, DOD's Basic Research investment has remained essentially constant since the S&T golden era of the 1960s and the space race. Unfortunately, this does not apply to the next level of R&D maturity, BA2 Applied Research. In both cases, however, the cost of a unit of research increased in the 1970s and 1980s at a much higher rate than the official DOD inflation factors, further eroding S&T buying power.

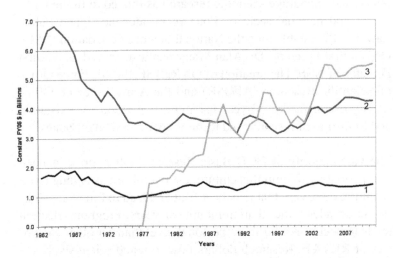

Figure 5. DOD S&T History (Constant FY-06 Dollars)
Adapted and reprinted with permission from DDR&E

Applied Research (BA2) and Advanced Technology Development (BA3) Culture – Federal Laboratories and Federally Funded R&D Centers (FFRDCs)

The metric for success in the academic scientific world is publication of a research paper in a respected journal. The metric for success in the engineering-centric world of Applied Research and beyond is final application of the technology within a deployed system to create a new, or improve an existing capability. Applied Research programs tend to begin a decade or more before production, and the Advanced Technology Development world tends to focus about five years out. The two-to-ten year window is too far from production and sales for significant for-profit investment interests and too close-in for most academic research interests. Thus the space is occupied primarily by non-profit activities: federal laboratories, Federally-Funded R&D Centers (FFRDCs), University Advanced Research Centers (UARCs) and a few private sector R&D companies. About 85 percent of BA3 dollars flow to the private sector. At this level of maturity, large systems integrators are just beginning to take interest in the work as a precursor to engineering development and production – so long as the bills are paid with federal dollars.

The falling BA 2 curve in Figure 5 graphically illustrates that Applied Research (6.2) is inherently vulnerable within the federal budget process. The apparent year-to-year instabilities in BA2 and BA3 reflect the impacts of short-term Congressional adds into these accounts. The actual PRESBUD requests for these accounts tend to be stable, with lower totals.

Approximately 85 percent of DOD's BA2 funding flows through federal laboratories (although the majority of BA2 dollars still ultimately flow to universities and R&D contractors). Federal laboratories are the most impotent of lobbies, lacking natural constituency outside their local Congressional Districts, lacking the legal ability to lobby directly, and lacking the knowledge of how to lobby effectively even if they were allowed to do so. Universities represent extremely powerful constituencies within virtually all Congressional Districts, but universities tend to concentrate their (highly extensive) lobbying efforts on Basic Research grants, which allow far greater freedom in program execution. In the private sector, even technology-centric companies tend to concentrate much more on BA3 than on BA2, which represents significantly larger project funding levels and, more importantly, nearer-term production profits.

The impact of funding reductions in BA2 is not felt for a decade or more, and it is not possible to quantify precisely the impact of technology that was never developed. When faced with present day budget shortfalls, an agency comptroller must weigh uncertain, inherently risky, ten-year-to-payoff Applied Research investment against very real near-term needs. In the case of DOD, those tradeoffs may include urgent manpower, fuel, and weapons budget shortfalls for ongoing conflicts. In large budget reductions, investment in future technology will lose almost 100 percent of the time. Even through the years of the Reagan defense buildup (the very best of times for the military-industrial complex), Applied Research investment remained essentially flat. In the case of the S&T investment of the Department of Navy, for which I was responsible, 6.2 Applied Research actually decreased 27 percent in constant dollars, as one of the bill payers for the "600 Ship Navy" initiative of the day. It is worthy to note that the 21st century Navy has 300 ships, and that technology investments not made in the 1980s arguably may have led to increased on-the-shelf capabilities today.

There is a hidden but no less important reason that BA2 is an inherently vulnerable account. The term "research" is highly ambiguous, and means vastly different things to different people. For those few individuals intimately acquainted with laboratory-style basic and applied research, the term refers specifically to "Technology Base" programs, i.e., those activities supported by BA1 and BA2 funding. For nearly everyone else on the planet, the term research is loosely used to describe any activity associated with Research, Development, Test and Evaluation (RDT&E). In the case of DOD, the actual Basic and Applied Research Programs (Technology Base) comprise only 7 percent of RDT&E. In other agencies, this disparity may be even greater.

A personal example: When I served as the first Director of the Naval Independent Research and Development (IR&D) in the early 1980s, a primary objective of the position was to assess, establish interactive communication with, and leverage industry IR&D investment. In today's dollars, the US industry IR&D investment at that time was far more than $5B annually. The assessment process included an annual formal review of the IR&D technical plans of every major DOD contractor, and an on-site review at company headquarters every third year. Industry senior executives proudly presented their research programs, frequently totaling many tens of millions of dollars. The assessment also included a determination of the appropriate RDT&E investment category, translated into DOD terminology. The assessments were absolutely consistent in their conclusions that the vast majority of the work referred to in private sector "research" was comparable in character with what DOD would classify as BA4 and BA5 advanced and engineering development activity. The IR&D investment assessed to be comparable to Basic and Applied Research (BA1 and BA2) was on the order of 3.5 percent, the bulk of which was conducted by fewer than 10 companies. Finally, these assessments were conducted at a time when vastly more dollars were available for long term investment than today.

A basic role of the private sector is to conduct the development and engineering necessary to produce the most capable systems at costs affordable to the American taxpayer. Given that role, for-profit companies focus their R&D on projects within one or two years of production and profitability. The meaning of "research" and the associated issue of perceived technical overlap actually is one of semantics, but it leads to both serious misunderstanding (with cultures unaware that they are talking past each other) and potentially catastrophic policy and budget decisions. To the Congressional Member or Staffer, understanding differences in the character of research conducted by the local university and the "research" conducted by the local for-profit contractor can be difficult at best. Those differences, however, are important to the actual tasks of the work at hand, and therefore need to be at least appreciated, if not understood, if one is to successfully navigate the system.

University lobbying efforts focus heavily on BA1 and research grants. Private industry focuses on BA4 and beyond – where the larger dollars are. In between, federal agencies can reduce internal budgets with minimal political ramifications and Congress can insert earmarks with minimum visibility or impact upon major systems acquisitions (and federal scientists and engineers normally cannot lobby for their causes). Not surprisingly, these facts lead to large numbers of Congressional earmarks in BA2 and BA3, and continuing budget instability as a way of life. On the other hand, the same invisibility, flexibility and ability to accept occasional failure allow federal laboratories using BA2 and BA3 funds to produce very innovative, nonlinear technologic successes, of which federal laboratory directors can be justifiably proud.

Engineering Development and Production Culture – Private Industry

On the opposite (acquisition) side of the "Valley of Death", at TRL 7 and beyond, a prototype technology has been demonstrated in an operational environment and in a configuration near to that of a planned operational system. Risk is no longer the technical question of "will it work," but a question of schedule and cost. By this point, there is very little "R," but lots of "D" in the R&D process, and production/profits are in sight. It is at this point where private industry takes the lead. The final product is no longer a technology demonstration, but a fielded capability.

Innovation versus Technology

Research and technology development tend to be linear and highly evolutionary in character. When comparing the latest model laptop computer to a ten-year-old model, the newer machine is faster, has a larger hard drive and more RAM, but represents in essence a predictable extrapolation of the technology of the earlier model. And an operator familiar with Windows 95™ or Windows 98™ can convert almost seamlessly to a current version of Windows™.

Innovation, on the other hand, tends to be nonlinear and disruptive in nature. Innovation occurs when an existing technology or process developed over time for a known use is applied, either singularly or in combination with other technologies and/or processes, to change a paradigm and produce an entirely new capability. Technology development follows predictable long-term schedules and budgets; innovation produces sudden changes, and often at very low cost.

Two favorite examples:

Students of S&T history know that the first defense-related national laboratory was the Naval Research Laboratory, established by Congress in 1923 with the strong advocacy of America's great inventor, Thomas Edison. Less well-known is that one of the early missions assigned by Congress to the fledgling NRL was in reaction to a catastrophic event that occurred before WWI – to locate icebergs so as to ensure that there would never be another Titanic disaster. NRL proceeded to invent SONAR to locate icebergs. Only later did a bright NRL scientist conclude that a technology with the capability of detecting icebergs also might be applicable to detection of submarines, and thereby created a war-winning capability in the Battle of the Atlantic during World War II.

Another example occurred during the 1950s at the Navy laboratory at China Lake, in the Mohave Desert of California. Most who have visited China Lake are aware of its famous "Radar Range," where the performance of many the world's most sophisticated radar systems is evaluated. An engineer aligning a microwave radar discovered that a chocolate bar in his pocket had absorbed the microwave radiation from the antenna, heated and melted. From this event came the realization that food could be heated very rapidly and efficiently by microwave energy, thus the world's first microwave oven. The first commercial microwave oven was named the "Radar Range®," in honor of the place where it was invented.

In both of these examples, technology developed for one use was applied in a different, and potentially an orthogonal way to create an entirely new capability. That defines innovation, and innovation happens most easily and most often in programs and climates where both risk and failure are acceptable (i.e., Applied Research and Advanced Technology Development-centric venues).

Technology Transition: 1950s – 1990s

The previous discussion points to a relatively ordered system of technology development that served the United States well for the half-century from the end of World War II until the 1990s. Academia focused on the time frame of ten years and beyond, developing the solid basic science floor upon which new technologies could be invented and developed. Federal and non-profit laboratories focused on the time frame from two to ten years, within which new, high risk, high payoff technologies could be investigated for feasibility, and demonstrated in realistic environments. Private industry took the handoff at a point about two years from production, confident that production and profitability were in sight after a bit more refinement and systems engineering. All in all, this represented a highly effective system, with each of the participants in the center of their respective comfort zones, and only minimal mission or technology overlap. This has changed significantly in the past two decades.

Paradigm Change #1- The Impact of the Strategic Defense Initiative (1986)

In 1984, President Reagan announced the creation of a massive new program called the Strategic Defense Initiative (SDI), more commonly known as "Star Wars", complete with a new, well-funded program office that still exists today as the Missile Defense Agency (MDA). As we shall discuss in the Bureaucracy 401 Chapter, budget decisions require a minimum of two years to implement, so the first major DOD budget impact of the SDI decision would appear in the 1986 DOD Budget. And as we shall discuss in the Bureaucracy 501 Chapter, there is no new money; all budget exercises are zero-sum. Figure 6 illustrates the far-reaching impact on the national S&T base of the Reagan SDI decision.

COMPARISON OF DOD S&T ACCOUNTS

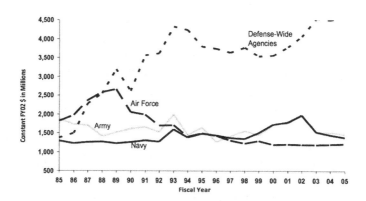

Figure 6. DoD S&T Budget Impact of SDI
Adapted and reprinted with permission from the Department of the Navy 2002 Potomac Institute for Policy Studies Publication # 02-01, "DOD Science and Technology Reinvigoration," conducted under ONR Grant # N00014-01-0326.

Prior to the SDI decision, the DOD staff and Defense Agencies (primarily DARPA) had small Science and Technology budgets relative to the military services. After the creation of the Strategic Defense Initiative Office (SDIO) in 1984, not only did the balance change within DOD as to where the dollars were spent, but the investment strategy also changed profoundly. Federal budgets are zero sum, and the DOD S&T top line increased only slightly in constant dollars after the SDI decision. Thus, the increase in DOD Agency spending, which now included both DARPA and SDIO, was offset by reduced military service spending, with the Air Force, as the unfortunate service most closely identified with space technology, contributing the largest share of the bill. Prior to 1986, DOD Agencies received less than a quarter of the total DOD S&T funding; since that time, they have received about half of the total. That is the case even with the apparent decrease in Defense Agency S&T investment after 1994. As we saw in the Bureaucracy 201 Chapter, the apparent reduction was, in reality, an artificial budget accounting change.

It is important to understand that this shift in S&T balance represented much more than a simple change in program execution from military services to DOD Agencies. Rather, it was an unintended paradigm shift in DOD S&T investment strategy. Using the analogy of the stock market, the S&T accounts are similar to the technology stock sector, with higher risks and potentially greater rewards than other investment options. The military services tend to diversify their S&T investment, with many small technology development tasks, just as most tech stock investors would do, in the hope that some will succeed. Defense Agencies, on the other hand, tend to focus their investment strategy on a smaller number of larger projects. With larger dollar investments, risk is less tolerable, programs are more conservative, and the resultant potential for innovation decreases.

A logical argument can be made that an even split of S&T dollars between services and Defense Agencies provides a balanced approach, with service investments being diversified and agency investments focused. My personal belief, based on more than four decades of conducting and managing technology transition, is that a diversified approach as conducted by the military services is a better strategy for S&T investment, especially when innovative technology solutions are a desired product. Personal opinions aside, Figure 6 shows that DOD moved to a fundamentally different DOD S&T investment strategy after the creation of SDIO.

Paradigm Change # 2- The "Peace Dividend (1991)"

After the fall of the Berlin Wall, the term "Peace Dividend" became a common phrase in defense circles. The assumption was made by the first Bush Administration, as well as by almost everyone else, that the end of the cold war signaled a time of international stability that would allow significant downsizing of the national security infrastructure without great risk. Although this assumption was later determined to be incorrect, it led to a number of irreversible decisions that changed forever the way technology was developed and transitioned in the United States. Most of these decisions were made simultaneously in 1991, and the synergistic impacts of multiple, seemingly unrelated policy changes are being felt strongly in the 21st Century.

One of the first impacts of the "Peace Dividend" was elimination of almost all discretionary spending for Applied Research. When budgets decrease, discretionary spending is reduced, and discretionary spending with an impact a decade or more away is always the first target. Prior to 1991, most federal laboratories had a "Lab Director's Fund," under various names, that enabled a director to allocate at his/her discretion a handful of dollars to investigate new high risk, high payoff ideas of the staff. The competition within such programs was fierce, and dollars rarely were awarded to any but the best and brightest. Concepts such as the feasibility of a Global Positioning System, laser guided weapons and reactive fragmentation began with the idea of a bright scientist or engineer and internal discretionary funding support. As would be expected, innovation and transition success from these kinds of programs was far above the norm. The loss of Lab Director's Funds and the consequent loss of innovation was a high cost of the Peace Dividend.

A second impact of the Peace Dividend was the privatization of much of the federal R&D infrastructure. As was discussed, most private industry executives, administration officials, Members of Congress and much of the general public believed honestly that American industry was conducting billions of dollars worth of basic and applied research, not realizing that what was known as research in the industry sector would be considered higher category development by the Science and Technology community. From this perspective, it is a completely logical assumption that the federal R&D infrastructure could be downsized significantly, and that the private sector could maintain the national technology base. The fallacy of the assumption, however, was that US industry does not reward an investment in R&D with a ten-year timeline before profitability, even in the best of times. In a free market system, the ten-year space must be occupied by federal and non-profit entities.

Fallacious assumptions notwithstanding, the decision was made by both the Republican and Democratic Administrations to downsize the federal infrastructure. As is almost always the case in a bureaucracy, this was not done by a thorough assessment of long term federal requirements followed by surgical reductions of expendable functions, but by the simplest method – encouraging indiscriminate early retirements. To "sweeten the pot," career civil servants were offered buyouts of $25,000 to leave their positions. The unintended consequence to the national Science and Technology base was severe, but the inherent lag time for S&T impact has masked the problem for a decade or more.

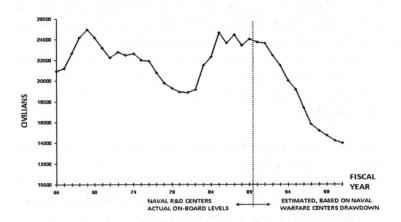

Figure 7. Naval Laboratory and Warfare Center Civilian Personnel Levels

Adapted and Reprinted with permission from the Department of the Navy 2002 Potomac Institute for Policy Studies Publication # 02-01, "DOD Science and Technology Reinvigoration," conducted under ONR Grant # N00014-01-0326.

The Figure 7 timeline begins in 1964 and follows the federal laboratory civilian end strength to the turn of the century, illustrating the impacts of the space race, Reagan defense buildup and 1990s federal downsizing decision. It uses the Navy system as the case study only because Navy had the most complete data base. The chart is similar whether Department of Energy, NASA or other military service laboratories are illustrated as examples. To understand the message completely, the chart must be considered over four decades.

President Kennedy's announcement of the national goal to land an American on the moon and return him safely to earth before 1970 launched what was to become a Science and Technology golden age for the United States. The President's timing was outstanding. Although he did not live to see the maturation of his vision, the cause captured both the imagination of the American people as a whole, as well as the imagination of a young and talented baby-boom generation in particular. This was a generation born after WWII and raised in the Eisenhower years, with vague recollections of Korea, but vivid memories of Sputnik, and the Berlin and Cuban Missile Crises. For this generation, a career in science offered the ability to participate in a great and exciting adventure and serve the nation at the same time. This was made possible by a sufficient level of national S&T investment. In the specific case of the Department of Navy (DON), its growing 1962 Applied Research (6.2) budget was three times larger than the current PRESBUD request for the same account.

A fact of far less nobility, but of great significance in the latter half of the decade was the fact that male scientists graduating with BS or advanced degrees, as the oldest in the draft pool, were highly vulnerable to be drafted and sent to combat in the nation's most unpopular war. The attractiveness of occupational deferments for scientists in federal laboratories and a downturn in private sector hiring of scientists and engineers (S&Es) as NASA neared its lunar goal combined with grand causes and patriotism to create a buyer's market for the Civil Service, an opportunity to select the best of an exceptionally talented pool of young professionals. For both good and bad reasons, scientists and engineers entered federal service in great numbers from 1964-1968.

By the 1970s, the climate had changed radically. Federal employment, and defense employment in particular, was viewed with less respect, and the morale of workers sagged. Federal laboratories began a period of minimal new hiring, low to moderate attrition, and a talented work force entering middle age. Military service S&T spending began a slow, steady decline that continued through the end of the century. DOD S&T investment remained relatively constant through the 1980s and 1990s, but with a significant funding migration to Defense Agencies, as discussed earlier.

In the 1980s, the federal government, and the DOD more specifically, began to hire once again. Two things were very different, however. In the 1960s, the best and brightest could either work in a federal laboratory with a draft deferment, or could fight in the Viet Nam War. Not surprisingly, most chose a deferment. In the 1980s, the best and brightest could choose between federal employment – at moderate pay – and the emerging computer and information technology industry – at high pay. Also not surprisingly, most chose higher pay. Thus, even though Figure 7 indicates that the federal workforce was rebuilt in the 1980s, it does not show that the average new employee of the 1980s was not the talent equivalent of the 1960s.

A more subtle difference is discovered if one compares the BA2 Applied Research curve in Figure 5 to the manpower graph of Figure 7. From 1964-1980, the shapes of the two curves are essentially identical, indicating that scientists and engineers hired during the period were given Applied Research assignments in their early careers. There is no agreement in the curves, however, in the 1980s, when new hires increased but Applied Research decreased. The incoming new staff, therefore, did not work primarily on S&T projects. Instead, they worked as project managers and budget analysts more than as scientists and engineers, and thus did not represent a functional replacement for the 1960s generation.

This leads to the most serious unintended consequence of the federal downsizing and privatization initiatives of the 1990s. Civil Service members were offered a $25,000 buyout as an incentive to retire. The population that accepted retirement incentives in greatest numbers was the workforce with 30 years or more of service – the exceptionally talented generation hired in the 1960s. Even more importantly, they represented the collective federal R&D experience and institutional memory.

Students of WWII history will recall that the Battle of Midway in May 1942 was the turning point in the War in the Pacific. The Japanese Empire was unable to recover from the defeat, not because of the loss of four carriers and their aircraft, but because of the loss of their irreplaceable experienced pilots. Talent and equipment are difficult to replace, but not impossible. The lessons of experience, however, once lost, often must be relearned by the painful process of repeating the mistakes of the past.

The dramatic downturn in numbers of scientists and engineers in DOD laboratories and the parallel downturn in DOD S&T budgets led to the next logical step – DOD laboratory consolidation. The Naval civilian personnel drawdown shown in Figure 7 was accompanied by the abolishment of the position of Director of Navy Laboratories, and transfer of the four Naval Warfare Centers to the Naval Systems Commands. Because the focus of the Systems Commands was on acquisition rather than technology, S&T in the Warfare Centers naturally declined. Within Navy, only the Naval Research Laboratory, in the direct chain-of-command of the Chief of Naval Research, fully maintained its S&T focus. Similarly, the Air Force and Army consolidated into single service laboratory structures, with former independent laboratories becoming divisions. A detailed discussion of the Naval laboratory history can be found in Appendix A.

Paradigm Change # 3- The Loss of Industry IR&D

Perhaps the most serious negative change to the national technology base in 1991 was the least noticed – the modification in the IR&D law. PL-914-41, Section 203, of the 1971 Military Personnel Authorization, provided for private industry recovery of Independent Research and Development (IR&D) expenses as general and administrative overhead, for building of the future business and technology base. Companies with IR&D programs in excess of $4M were required (1) to submit a technical plan describing each technical project, which the DOD would evaluate for "potential military relationship;" (2) to negotiate an agreement with the DOD which established an IR&D ceiling for cost recovery (Note: Most companies exceeded the cost recovery ceiling each year, with company dollars paying as much as one-third of the total IR&D.); and (3) to present an on-site review of its IR&D program to the DOD at least once every three years.[15] In December 1991, responding to pressure from industry to simplify the process and to allow full recovery of IR&D expenses, Congress passed PL-102-190, which stated that "independent R&D and bid and proposal costs of DOD contractors shall be allowable as indirect costs on covered contracts to the extent that such costs are allocable, reasonable, and not otherwise unallowable by law or under the Federal Acquisition (FAR)." The legislation allowed full recovery of IR&D expenses and negated requirements for IR&D ceiling negotiations with DOD (industry's primary goal in pursuing the legislation), but also negated the requirement for industry reporting and DOD review and oversight of IR&D.[16]

From a national technology base perspective, PL-102-90 produced two huge, unintended, and negative consequences. First, it allowed (viz.- effectively encouraged) industry to reduce overhead rates by reducing IR&D investment. IR&D budgets shrank almost instantly to less than half of their levels before the law change, and the character of IR&D work became nearer-term [more akin to Bid-and-Proposal (B&P) work] as the substantial 1980s defense budget dropped to the more austere 1990s levels. Second, the DOD and industry lost a forcing function to encourage and assure access to each other's R&D, ending a period of many years of mutually advantageous technical communication and leverage between the public and private sectors. Ironically, although demands for leverage of private sector technology have increased steadily throughout the nearly two decades following passage of PL-102-90, private sector technology development has become, with few exceptions, far less visible to the federal government.

The net impact of these systemic changes occurring almost simultaneously led to a dramatic, yet largely unperceived shift in national paradigm for development and transition of technology. Loss of federal S&T corporate memory and S&T focus is very important for the health of the national technology base. Although 85 percent of federal S&T dollars are spent in the private sector, almost 100 percent of the early stage R&D dollars are federal. In fact, two separate internal studies that I commissioned in the late 1990s found that the federal share of the national Basic Research investment was more than 98 percent of the total, and the federal share was far above 90 percent for both Applied Research and Advanced Development. Not surprisingly, industry IR&D and other private sector R&D investment shares of the costs grow higher and finally dominate as the time to production and profit grows shorter.

While the reduction in federal investment made industry IR&D more important than ever to the health of the national technology base, simultaneous passage of PL-102-90 led to dramatic decreases in IR&D investment. With fewer dollars to spend, the R&D became more near-term and conservative (i.e., B&P character). More significantly, the large company focus shifted from internal technology development to technology company acquisition, buying small companies to acquire their technology rather than developing the same technology in-house.

Returning to the strategic picture, the federal laboratory downsizing led to the availability of a large number of exceptionally bright scientists and engineers, most in their productive mid-fifties that were still too young and too energetic to retire. Many of these scientists and engineers (S&Es) formed or joined small technology companies and continued previous work in their respective areas of expertise. Others focused on the emerging private sector information technology boom of the 1990s. In both cases, the national system enabling and encouraging innovation has evolved since 1991 from the federal and non-profit sector to small technology companies.

For those managing the small companies, lifetime financial security is assured when their companies are acquired by larger firms. Thus a major incentive for small technology companies is to develop a suite of technologies, at least one of which will become so desirable to a large systems integrator that the small company will be acquired for the technology. An unfortunate downside for the nation of such a system is that development of those technologies not of interest to the larger company is unlikely to continue. This leads to many lost opportunities – innovative ideas of the small company may disappear forever –and also to far higher costs for technology development. Should a small company developing a number of creative technologies be acquired because of interest in only one technology or system, the cost of a unit of technology development increases with every idea that is discarded.

These fundamental changes in the innovation paradigm create a new set of requirements for all parties involved in the acquisition process. The first is to connect innovators and users. The federal government and large systems integrators have minimal knowledge of small companies that may be developing technology solutions of great interest, and the small companies have even less idea who to call in government or industry to market their product. The federal IR&D program offices performed this function prior to 1991, but lost most of the ability to make the connections after the law changed. Organizations are needed, federal or non-profit, that specialize in enabling those connections and in the requisite technology bridge-building.

Another major requirement of the new innovation/transition paradigm is the effective integration of Small Business Innovation Research (SBIR), and Small Business Technology Transfer (STTR) planning with federal systems acquisition planning. SBIR, established as a formal program 25 years ago and administered by 12 federal agencies, has grown from a small-dollar program of minimal consequence to a multi-billion dollar annual investment, far too large to be ignored by the national R&D community. Not surprisingly, DOD has the largest SBIR investment, currently on the order of $1.5B. For detailed SBIR/STTR information, see www.sbir.gov and www.dodsbir.net.

In the past, SBIR has operated largely outside the mainstream federal technology transition and acquisition processes. With the center of innovation moving from federal laboratories to small technology companies, SBIR has the potential to become one of the system's most vital components in the future. For this to occur, two things must change:

First, the SBIR focus must shift from numbers of Phase I and Phase II awards as a metric for success to numbers of successful transitions to Phase III, the point at which the program continues forward with other than SBIR dollars. Every person associated with SBIR for any length of time can name a long list of companies that survive by moving from SBIR Phase I to Phase II, then back to Phase I and II, then back ad infinitum, offering new SBIR proposals but never producing a useful product or transitioning a capability. A cottage industry even exists to assist and train companies in the fine art of SBIR Phase I and II proposal development. When the metric for success is technology insertion into a system, things change overnight.

Second, almost all successful technology transition occurs when technology solutions are pulled forward by meeting a user's requirement rather than pushed by a technology's excellence. Unfortunately, most federal agency SBIR Program Offices reside in the S&T side of the agency, and many are completely unaware of the program acquisition strategy of their agency. Rarely did a week go by in my five years at the Institute for Defense and Homeland Security without one or more calls from small company executives to state both that they were nearing completion of an SBIR Phase II contract and needed guidance on how to approach Phase III, and that the agency SBIR manager did not know how to advise them. Unfortunately, the standard answer was that they were many years too late in raising the transition question. Programming funds in the federal system requires two years as an absolute minimum. To be effective, Phase III transition planning should begin no later than – and ideally, before – Phase I program execution begins.

After I discussed this topic at a recent SBIR conference, a offline conversation revealed that the SBIR Program Manager of a very large federal agency did not know a single person in the agency's acquisition community. This kind of issue is more a fault of the system than of an individual, and can be resolved simply by transfer of SBIR oversight from the agency's technology chain-of-command to the acquisition side.

The same arguments that are made for connecting SBIR more closely to user-driven requirements can apply equally well to the DOD Manufacturing Technology (MANTECH) Program. Both programs can make legitimate cases that they employ requirements-driven processes already, but the requirements are driven generally from the mid-level, and in most cases lack the strategic perspective of the agency's top-down acquisition planning.

There is a potential danger of moving to the opposite extreme for both SBIR and MANTECH; should they become overly focused, they turn into support programs for near-term acquisition programs. At worst, they become hidden funding sources for acquisition shortfalls. Fortunately, there is a happy medium. SBIR, STTR and MANTECH programs that address known capability shortfalls, but with independence in program execution, allow and encourage innovation in the respective technical approaches.

The final new requirement and new opportunity from the evolving technology transition and innovation paradigm is to increase emphasis on university-based Applied Research and Advanced Development. Historically, universities have concentrated on Basic Research, with capability payoffs more than a decade away. Encouraging universities to engage in research and technology in the five-to-ten year timeline not only fills a widening technology personnel void, but also adds the powerful academic constituency to those lobbying for Applied Research funding.

BUREAUCRACY 401
THE PEOPLE OF THE BUREAUCRACY

Understanding the Federal System

The federal R&D bureaucracy consists of three distinct cultures: political appointees, military officers and career civilians. These cultures have complementary strengths and weaknesses, as well as significantly different agendas. As expected, the system operates best when all three work in harmony, exploiting the synergy of diversity coupled with talent. This chapter explores the value sets, strengths and weaknesses of each of the three cultures. To operate effectively in the federal space, one must understand which culture he/she is addressing. The three are uniquely different, perhaps far more than the uninitiated might expect.

The Federal Culture

Political Appointees
Otto Von Bismarck observed that "Laws are like sausages, it is better not to see them being made." For many, it is a fascinating exercise to watch the Congressional process move forward, as members who want to "do the right thing" can only do so for one term, unless they are reelected. Their reelection is only secure when they adequately "take care of" their constituents, which usually means bringing federal dollars into their respective districts. Thus "the right thing" decision frequently must be made in a political context, in which the desires and needs of the constituent few can become more important than those of the non-constituent many. Lest the reader jump to the conclusion that such a system is inherently corrupt and far beyond repair, the intrinsic checks and balances historically have worked rather well. Even though nearly every American can recount a favorite anecdote of a Congressional snafu or scandal, the competing special interests of over 500 congressional districts create a natural tension that (most of the time) keeps the system in equilibrium.

It is from this world that most federal political appointees enter the system. Like all federal employees, their fundamental role is one of public service, but this is public service as contextualized within the agenda of the political administration that the appointees represent. The typical appointee can usually be counted upon to exhibit a number highly predictable characteristics, these include:

- In charge.
- Highly talented.
- Boundless enthusiasm and optimism.
- Political or private sector mindset.
- Near-term focus.
- Variable experience level.
- Distrust of non-appointees (civilian and military).
- Specific, sometimes narrow agendas.
- Importance of image.

Let us consider each of these in turn.

In charge
Appointees are, by design and law, the final authority for major money and policy decisions. The weaker appointees usually will feel the need to make a point many times and in various ways. Stronger ones will assume correctly that their career colleagues will accept this fact as an inherent characteristic of the system.

Highly talented
Appointees, regardless of background, can be counted upon to be talented and energetic. Senior positions directly reflect upon the Administration that they serve, and they generally are chosen with care. Support of the Administration's policies is required, but competence and thoughtful decision-making is favored in senior executives over blind obedience. Note: This may not be the case for more junior (GS 13-15 level) appointees, for whom the appointment may be a reward for faithful party or campaign support.

Boundless enthusiasm and optimism
Like the politicians that gave them professional life, appointees can be counted upon to be eternally optimistic and fiercely protective of the Administration's positions on issues of importance. In the words of Dr. James Colvard, a superb federal executive who served in both career and appointee roles and appreciates the inherent strengths and weaknesses of both, "Washington is the only place where one [data] point can represent a trend, and two points a tradition."

Political or private sector mindset
This characteristic can be highly frustrating to career civilian and military executives, but it represents a fundamental strength of the appointment system. Each culture believes it understands much about the other two, but in reality this mutual understanding does not exist. Appointees bring with them, from the receiving end, an understanding of the non-federal world and a first-hand appreciation of the ramifications of bad government decisions. This is the American public culture that career public servants are charged to serve, but with whom they sometimes lose touch.

Near-term focus
Senior appointees accept significant reductions in pay from their positions in the private sector to come to government service. Their average appointee tenure is on the order of 18 months, after which they are likely to reengage in positions of higher pay and influence on the outside. As we shall see later, the minimum time for development of an internal program initiative is 24 months (driven by the Congressional appropriation process). Thus the appointee timeline is inherently in conflict with the federal budget. Initiatives requiring multiple years to bear fruit tend to be of lower interest, especially when near-term dollars are necessary for success. Programs that pay up front and allow someone else to later take credit are usually highly unpopular.

Variable experience level
This is, in my opinion, the single greatest weakness of the appointee system. Experience is a commodity that can be obtained only with time, through lessons learned in observing one's own – and others' – successes and failures. Many senior appointees are mid- and late career executives who enter public service for the best of reasons – to offer their talents and experience to their country. Such people usually are secure enough in their abilities to recognize their own vulnerabilities. As a rule, they tend to consider the advice of others who may understand the intricacies and specific issues of the federal system better than themselves.

A common source of senior appointees, however, is the pool of young Congressional or personal staffers, who often bring exceptional talent but a narrow experience base to a decision-making position. The mid-thirties members of this culture are generally one or two decades younger than the senior career civilians and military officers around them. A large ego is an essential requirement for almost all senior positions (career or appointee), and many younger executives find it necessary to demonstrate their authority. At worst, this can lead to discounting very good advice and ignoring important lessons of history. To reiterate for emphasis: the issue is *not* of talent, but of experience. As someone who occupied senior positions at a relatively young age, I understand this mindset – and have my own personal set of mistakes and lessons learned as a result.

Distrust of non-appointees (civilian and military)
There is plenty of blame to pass on all sides of the trust issue. Many senior appointees enter their jobs in the absolute certainty that the resident career staff will work actively to maintain the *status quo* and to undermine the interests of the Administration. This can be true, and both sides can establish self-fulfilling prophecies of mistrust and failure. Political rhetoric inevitably promises to clean up the "bloated bureaucracy" and get control of the "faceless bureaucrats", but administrations that carry out their agendas

most successfully tend to work within the established system and build coalitions with (sometimes reluctant) career personnel as necessary allies.

Specific, sometimes narrow agendas
Appointees are put in place by an Administration specifically to ensure that decisions and programs of the agency support the policies of that Administration. Career employees understand this, but also understand that administrations and agendas will change, and thus will work to minimize the impact of long-term policy decisions. At best, all sides understand the need for and respect the perspectives of the others. At worst, the appointee's agenda is narrow and highly personal. In such cases, the parties engage in an extended battle of wills, which usually damages the interests of all.

Importance of image
A few years ago, television commercials for a major camera company featured a famous athlete and the quote: "Image is everything!" Just as appearance and style are critical to the election of political candidates, they are equally important to those they appoint. The short average tenure of appointees ensures that most will not see the end product of their efforts. Their performance, therefore, must be based on real-time actions. A typical appointee prefers to focus on high profile initiatives with near-term payoff and the appearance of change and rapid progress.

Military Officers
In contrast– characteristics of Military Officers (i.e., the second culture) are rather different. These characteristics include:

- Honest, highly patriotic, highly dedicated.
- 24-36 month focus.
- Chain-of-command oriented – highly rank-conscious.
- Structured career – specific positions and awards.
- Culturally optimistic.
- Highly social, but within the military family.
- Autocratic mindset – opposite of bureaucratic.
- Changing retirement paradigm – transition to Civil Service.

It is personally gratifying to see our nation treat members of the military, and especially those who put their lives at risk, with admiration and respect. This was not the case in the 1970s, when a generation of patriotic Americans was maligned because they chose to serve. The career military represents a different culture, one that is frequently misunderstood by those looking from the outside. Within the federal bureaucracy, however, the military mindset is the most easily understood, and its decisions the most straightforward and predictable. On the other hand, the military model for decision-making is not wholly compatible with bureaucratic processes. We shall see why as we review the characteristics of the senior military members of the bureaucracy, in turn.

Honest, highly patriotic, highly dedicated
It is rare that a military officer reaches the grade of O-6 or above (Captain or Admiral in the Navy, Colonel or General in the other Services) without being honest, patriotic and dedicated. By this point in their careers, character and leadership skills have been tested multiple times, often under pressure. A few bad apples may make it through the process, but the great majority of senior officers can be counted on to represent the best of our culture.

24-36 month focus
While an appointee might remain for 18 months or so, senior military leaders will be in place for two or three years. Consequently, their focus tends to be of a time frame long enough to complete the task of a predecessor or to handoff a new initiative to a successor. Maintaining continuity and a smooth transfer of power thus are important parts of the role of the military.

Chain-of-command oriented – highly rank-conscious
Members of the military are trained from the beginning to obey orders of a superior. As such, the rank of another military member relative to your own is important; so important, in fact, that the rank is displayed externally for all to see. When two flag officers of equal rank are to have a telephone conversation, the officer with less time in grade places the call, even when the seniority difference is only slight. This is a very strange system to most civil-

ians, who wear no such external signs of rank, and prefer a more casual, collegial atmosphere. When flag or general officer rank is achieved, it represents a rite-of-passage within the military culture generally not understood or appreciated by the other two cultures.

Structured career – specific positions and awards
Within military culture, the path "up or out" is highly structured. For a young officer beginning a career as an Army second lieutenant or Navy ensign, the way ahead is defined within relatively narrow boundaries. The expected number of years at each grade level is known, as is the expected award at the end of each assignment. An earlier than normal rise to the next grade and/or a higher than normal award is a very good sign of things to come, and a slower than normal rise or a lesser award is a solid indicator for the individual to plan for an early departure from the service. Career civilians and appointees have no such structure, nor do they appreciate its importance within the military.

Culturally optimistic
The "glass half full" answer is expected when a question is asked in public to any member of the military. The program will be successful and all objectives will be achieved. If the normally rhetorical "How are you doing?" greeting is given to a service member with a raging cold, complete with fever and chills, the most likely answer will be a variant of "It's a great (Navy, Army, Air Force or Marine Corps) day!", complete with a big smile and a warm handshake. Military members pride themselves on their ability to excel even in the face of severe influenza, nausea and/or diarrhea. This leads frequently to a situation in which their friends and office mates are given the same opportunity to excel in the days ahead.

Highly social, but within the military family
Social events are an important part of military culture, and tend to reinforce lifetime bonding of friends with shared experiences. Within the social structure, the roles of all, including family members, are well defined. The primary interaction tends to occur among the military members, in a style that appears rigid and

formal to those on the outside. Civilian colleagues are invited to participate when they are a part of the organization, but usually not otherwise.

A military approach to socializing occurred in the Pentagon when it was reported to an admiral that morale appeared to be sagging among the administrative personnel. The admiral's senior staff followed up with a classic military solution – to schedule a party for the organization to demonstrate to all just how important every member of the administrative staff was to the success of the organization as a whole. The decision was made and the date was set. Then the administrative staff received a new assignment to organize, supply food, and clean up after the party in their honor!

User perspective. Requirements-driven
Above all else, the military member of the team brings the vital perspective of the person who has "been there", possibly at great personal risk, and knows first-hand what is needed. In the case of defense-related R&D, military members represent the ultimate customer, and the reason that the rest of us are working. Scientists and engineers are notorious perfectionists, always wanting techniques or technology to perform just a bit better, or to add the last bit of gold plating. But in the no-nonsense words of Admiral Sergey Gorshkov, a former Commander-in-Chief of the Soviet Navy, "Better is the enemy of good enough."

On the other hand, career civilians and appointees, especially senior technical experts, are put in place to challenge the status quo and to ensure that "good enough" today will still be good enough tomorrow. In the early days of WWII, American pilots fought and many died in desperate battles between their P-39 and P-40 fighter aircraft and superior Japanese and German machines, in part because Army Air Corps planners decided that superchargers (enabling high altitude performance) were not required for their projected missions.[17] What was adequate in 1938 was obsolescent by early 1942. Sometimes, "good enough" isn't good enough.

Autocratic mindset – opposite of bureaucratic
In a military command, the senior officer is in charge. In the heat of battle, decisions must be made quickly to achieve victory, and orders are expected to be obeyed without question. In a bureaucracy, a large set of people of equal rank and varied, frequently opposing interests is collectively in charge – meaning that no single individual is truly in command. This can be highly frustrating to a military officer in a bureaucratic system, who at worst may retreat into an inflexible and highly risk-averse posture, even with the understanding that indecision can be far worse than a bad decision.

Constant change is a basic characteristic of the federal bureaucracy. In a bureaucratic battle, there are scores of constantly moving parts, including new personalities, unprogrammed budget requirements and political issues. As a result, the more controversial the decision, the later it should be made – with the maximum amount of information in hand, and still remaining as flexible as possible. This is a tall order, especially for a senior military officer. For some of the best military bureaucrats, "Semper Gumby" (metaphorically- always flexible, recalling the bendable, but not breakable green claymation figure of the 1960s) is a rallying cry, no matter how inconsistent with their training. For those who can remain flexible, a Pentagon tour will be enlightening and considerably more enjoyable than expected. For those who cannot, and there are many, a tour in the Pentagon will seem to last forever.

Changing retirement paradigm – transition to Civil Service
Prior to the year 2000, if a member of the military services retired and became a career civil servant, the retiree was unable to "double dip" from the government. Maximum pay was limited to the higher of the Civil Service or military retirement pay, but the retiree could not receive both. Although this policy put retired military and retired career civil servants on equal footing, it served as a huge disincentive for military retirees to continue in a Civil Service career, and so in most cases their expertise was lost the federal government.

In the FY-00 Defense Authorization (PL-106-65), Congress removed the double-dipping penalty for military retirees.[18] This was good news from the perspective of maintaining corporate memory, as it provided a bridge for capable former military personnel to maintain the Civil Service experience base as the 1960s generation of scientists and engineers was exiting. However, as so often happens, the unintended consequences can be very significant.

Transition to Civil Service after a 20-to-30 year military career became a highly desirable option, and frequently an easy one to implement. I observed numerous occasions of military officers (O-4 and above) working actively to convert their current military position to civilian status and then to apply for the position, for which they were guaranteed to be highly qualified. An especially attractive option was for a colonel or Navy captain to compete for and to be selected to a civilian Senior Executive Service (SES) position, which allowed the O-6 to achieve flag rank (O-7 equivalent or above) as a civilian, even though they had been unable to achieve that rank and rite of passage within the military system. Within DOD and the services, selecting and/or approving officials were often flag officers themselves. For the first few years after double-dipping was allowed, I watched the process for DOD SES selections and made mental notes of the impact of the change. During one period I followed the selection processes of more than a dozen SES vacancies in DOD and Service headquarters; in each case a retiring O-6 was selected. It is important to add that all selectees were qualified, and several have become outstanding civil servants. Cultural diversity, however, strengthens a workforce and minimizes organizational biases in the same manner as racial, ethnic and gender diversity.

There are two especially negative downsides of incentivizing military retirees to transition to Civil Service. One obvious disadvantage is the limitation of higher grade (particularly GS-15 and SES) advancement opportunities for career civil servants. This will be discussed in more detail in the next section.

The other is far less obvious, but potentially more serious in the long term. An inherent strength of military culture is that it is highly rank-conscious; an inherent strength of the civilian culture is that it is not. A personal observation is that very few military officers who transition to Civil Service are able to fully shed either their military mindset or their former military rank in the execution of their civilian duties. I recall one very capable O-5 staff officer who transitioned to a GS-14 (equivalent rank) civilian position, then later was promoted to GS-15 (O-6 equivalent rank). Despite the civilian promotion, the individual continued to operate mentally as an O-5 equivalent staff officer, and to this day is unable to interact with colonels or Navy captains as peers. On the other end, the active duty colonels and captains know equally well of the former military rank and continue to give that individual a level of attention and respect befitting a commander or lieutenant colonel.

This phenomenon is especially serious for those fortunate colonels and Navy captains who are promoted to the Senior Executive Service. SES members are charged with the responsibility of serving alongside – and sometimes confronting – generals and admirals as peers rather than as superior officers. Even for those former O-6s that succeed in making this mental transition to flag rank, it is an uphill battle; the flag and general officers with whom they serve will be well aware of their former military rank. Unfortunately, a number do not succeed, and as a result the inherent checks and balances afforded by the cultural diversity of the system are compromised.

Career Civilians

Last, but certainly not least, we come to the culture of career civilians. Characteristics of this culture include:

- Honest, highly patriotic and dedicated.
- Not motivated by money.
- Long term focus.
- Culturally pessimistic.
- Frequently distrustful of appointees.

- Fiercely protective of federal decision authority.
- Appearances and style – relatively unimportant.
- Talented, but not necessarily creative.
- Evolving military presence in the culture.

Despite a positive bias based upon an association with this group for more than for four decades, I must admit that "my people" on occasion have worked hard to earn the title of "faceless bureaucrat." Thankfully, faceless bureaucrats become increasingly rare as the pay grade increases, and the title applies infrequently at the senior levels of GS-15 and above. The career civilian model for decision-making is the essence of bureaucratic processes. We shall see why as we review the specific characteristics of the senior career civilian members of the bureaucracy.

Honest, highly patriotic and dedicated
Similar to the military system, it is rare that a career civilian reaches a senior position without being honest, patriotic and dedicated, with one exception. A poorly performing Senior Executive Service member can be removed from a position of influence in short order, but General Schedule (GS) employees arguably have the highest job security on the planet. A skillful, but not particularly dedicated GS-15 can use talent to advance to a desired position, and then perform just well enough to maintain a "fully satisfactory" rating and burrow for a long and comfortable career. Such people are rare at GS-14/15 levels, but examples do exist. Progressively more examples can be found at increasingly lower pay grades. At intermediate grade levels, the ability exists to disappear and become "faceless" in the enormous federal system.

Not motivated by money
For senior federal employees, the unsurpassed US Civil Service job security comes at a price – a far lower salary than for positions of comparable responsibility on the outside. While not necessarily true for lower and middle grades, those for whom salary level is a high priority rarely work in senior government positions, federal or otherwise. Almost any federal senior executive can provide anecdotes of unsolicited offers on the outside,

often for twofold or greater increases in pay. What serves as motivators for senior federal employees, however, are high job satisfaction and an understanding that the contribution is a genuine public service. As noted above, this may not always be true for lower level federal employees.

Long term focus
Career employees have the task of providing long term stability for a system within which players from the other two cultures are constantly changing. This provides and upside of federal job tenure to offset the "retired on the job" downside discussed above, as well it serves a strong forcing function to ensure that the long term view is always considered. The tenure of a typical senior civil servant is at least five years, and often much longer. When bad decisions are made, the career staff is left to clean up the fallout. The incentive to work hard to eliminate – or at least to minimize – bad decisions becomes a matter of simple self interest.

Culturally pessimistic
For appointees and military officers, the expected answer is "yes", regardless of the question. For career executives, the standard first answer is "no", with an occasional "maybe" thrown in. It is the role of the career bureaucrat to be the naysayer. He/she must search for every technical reason the idea won't work, assess the probabilities of every potential Act of God that could jeopardize success, and develop future alternative strategies to employ when things go awry, as they almost surely will in every program. In short, while the appointees declare great success on day one, and the military leaders put on the official face of optimism, the bureaucrat serves as a counterbalance to make sure all contingencies are considered. In the folksy terms of the old country church, it's the job of the career bureaucrat to serve as the "aginner." The important point to recognize is that with a two-thirds majority of the players being inherently over-optimistic, the other one-third needs to be a vocal minority and play the "Whatever the plan is, I'm agin it!" role to achieve overall objectivity, balance and a rational assessment of alternative approaches.

Frequently distrustful of appointees
Especially with the change of presidential administrations, many appointees will come into their positions convinced that intransigent career bureaucrats will do everything in their power to maintain status quo and to thwart the righteous aims of the new administration. Senior career bureaucrats know this all too well, having experienced the transfer of power and authority many times before, and may themselves help to create a self-fulfilling prophecy of mutual distrust. Trust usually does come, however, but only with time.

Fiercely protective of federal decision authority
I have been asked many times by consultants and small companies how they can assist the Federal Government in making wise program and policy decisions. The answer, if career bureaucrats have anything to do with it, is "No way!" Federal executives view their role as a sacred public trust and would see delegation of any function related to federal decision authority as a serious breach of that trust. Good bureaucrats will encourage and welcome factual input to assist in decision-making, but will never knowingly allow major decisions to be made or unduly influenced from outside the system.

Appearances and style – relatively unimportant
In this case, the career executive is the antithesis of the appointed official, for whom style may be of equal or greater importance than substance. The career bureaucrat must deal with the consequences of short-term plans and shallow motivations, and is far more interested in facts and long term results than appearance. Unfortunately, this does not often lead to colorful and exciting bureaucrats, and most of the faces seen by the Congress or the press are appointed officials or military officers. Career bureaucrats neither stir the emotions nor make very good poster children.

On August 14, 1945, the Japanese people heard the voice of their Emperor Hirohito for the first time as he stated "… the war situation has developed not necessarily to Japan's advantage…" While His Majesty's declaration was true, and a classic political statement, it fell a bit short of describing the state of a nation on the brink of total collapse. A career bureaucrat making the same speech would include numerous statistics and probably would describe in great detail the devastation of firebombs and two nuclear attacks. The saying: "I became a bureaucrat because I didn't have the charisma to be an accountant!" applies more accurately than most of us would like to believe.

Talented, but not necessarily creative
Almost all career executives are talented; the federal promotion system has so many checks and balances that those without sufficient talent usually are weeded out along the way. Large bureaucracies tend to reward stability, and in most cases, neutrality. The best bureaucrats learn to be "creatively neutral," leading others to "do the right thing" in a consensus manner. However, creativity frequently brings with it an inherent factor of instability, which can be threatening within the system. A bureaucrat who becomes highly adept at performing a relatively stable and narrow, but important function can succeed quite well.

Evolving military presence in the culture
The federal Senior Executive Service culture is changing rapidly as an unintended consequence of two forcing functions. One was the influx of military retirees into the Civil Service discussed in the previous section. With very stiff competition from former military officers for senior positions, the easier way to fame and fortune for talented federal employees is to leave at mid-career, an option unintentionally enabled by the second forcing function – transition to a new retirement system – FERS.

In 1987, the generous Civil Service Retirement System (CSRS) was replaced by the apparently less generous Federal Employee Retirement System (FERS). Under CSRS, the longest-serving senior bureaucrats, most of whom spent four decades earning lower pay than their private sector counterparts, were rewarded for their financial sacrifice with outstanding job security and, for the golden years, a lifetime retirement pension of 60- 80 percent of the average of their highest three years of federal pay. CSRS exacted heavy penalties, however, for anyone who left the system before full retirement eligibility. As a result, most federal employees covered under CSRS did not leave federal service earlier than the usual minimum requirement – 55 years of age, and 25 or more years of service. In fact, I received multiple unsolicited offers to increase salary by a factor of two or more by moving to the private sector. All offers were refused, based at least partly upon the CSRS incentive to remain in the system.

The FERS system was designed to be similar to private sector retirement models, relying on matching employee contributions in tax-deferred retirement accounts and Social Security. The account is owned by the federal employee, and, unlike CSRS, there is no penalty for early retirement from the system. In theory, FERS lowers the costs to the American taxpayer in terms of total pension benefits.

As before, the most talented civil servants still will have attractive opportunities to leave at mid-career (GS-14/15) for much higher paying private sector positions. Unlike CSRS, however, there is no major penalty for leaving (or coming back into) federal service. For the employees who choose to remain inside, they will face stiff competition from O-6 and flag-level military retirees for future Senior Executive Service positions. For most, it is an unattractive prospect to remain inside for up to two decades (until full retirement) without a realistic possibility of promotion. The CSRS incentivized the "best and brightest" to remain in Civil Service for their entire careers. FERS, coupled with the influx of former military officers into Civil Service, incentivizes the best and brightest to leave federal service at age 40-50, potentially the most productive time of their careers, to accept higher-paying positions outside.

Military and Civilian Rank Equivalencies
Figure 8 shows the formal rank equivalencies between senior military and civilian ranks. Within the system, however, a well-defined "greater of equals" hierarchy exists. The greatest of equals is the executive level appointee civilian, who formally represents the position of the President and has final decision authority. Within the DOD, the next in line are military officers, who have formal command responsibility. The hierarchy is made clear through the policy that when military officers and senior civilians of equal

rank request vehicles or lodging, priority is given to the officer. Those who spend their full careers in the Civil Service accept this not only as a fact of life, but as necessary and appropriate within the military culture.

Top level policy and program decisions are made at the senior appointee and military four-star level. Discussions tend to focus on significant policy or political issues and very large programs, generally of hundreds of millions to billions of dollars in size.

The majority of decisions affecting specific programs and funding levels of ones to tens of millions in size are made by people in the second and third rows of the chart. This is an important fact to understand for most individuals or entities that are marketing programs to the federal system. In the end game, the successful program manager will be communicating in most cases with O-8 or O-9 level military officers and "club member" SES Tier II or III career civilians.

MILITARY AND CIVILIAN RANK EQUIVALENCIES

Military	Civilian
O-10 - General, Admiral	Executive Level Appointee
O-9 - Lieutenant General, Vice Admiral	SES Tier III
O-8 - Major General, Rear Admiral Upper Half (RADM)	SES Tier II
O-7 - Brigadier General, Rear Admiral Lower Half (RDML)	SES Tier I
O-6 - Colonel, Captain (CAPT)	GS-15
O-5 - Lt Colonel, Commander	GS-14
O-4 - Major, Lt Commander	GS-13
O-3 - Captain, Lieutenant	GS-12

Figure 8. Military and Civilian Rank Equivalencies

One-star generals/admirals and very senior O-6s, especially those who formally command large bases or organizations, may have on their staff senior civilians who are higher in formal rank. One example is the Naval Research Laboratory, whose Commanding Officer is a Navy captain and whose Director of Research is a Tier III career SES. Less secure officers (often the newest generals and admirals) frequently waste time and effort demonstrating to all who will listen that they are in command. The more secure officers, on the other hand, realize that having staff members senior to their own formal rank not only enhances their prestige, but may give them entrée to perquisites otherwise unavailable. One Naval SES who worked for such a captain found himself invited regularly to the captain's outside meetings, not as a tribute to his impressive technical expertise, but to the fact that Naval senior executives qualify for Navy vehicles and a driver, while the captain did not. New flag and general officers would do well to understand that senior civilians fully appreciate the fact that the military is in command and why that is so, and that they stand ready to support the military leadership.

It should be noted also that only a small subset of SES members are fully accepted by the senior military and appointee cultures as peers and trusted to be decision-makers, even though they might be, at least on paper, of equal rank. The SES members who also are "club members" can be identified as those (1) who personally make significant money decisions and/or (2) who are trusted to speak off-the-record on Capitol Hill on behalf of their respective agencies. Acceptance into this "club" is unrelated to formal SES rank (although a Tier 1 SES member would be rare). Instead, membership is related entirely to personal credibility and influence within the system.

BUREAUCRACY 501
DOD R&D PROGRAM AND BUDGET DEVELOPMENT

Almost every American citizen has thought, and perhaps commented on how slowly the wheels of the federal system turn, but few realize that the entire timeline is driven by the Congressional authorization and appropriation processes. Under the current system, the minimum time for a federal agency to establish a new program initiative is two years, and the actual timeline can be far longer.

To understand why the federal budget process is so laborious, it must be examined along the entire timeline from an initial great idea to the point of program execution with funding in hand. The DOD budget process is known as the Planning, Programming, Budgeting and Execution Process, or PPBE. The subject may be dry as sand, but public or private sector individuals who understand federal budget fundamentals – and especially who controls budget decision at different points on the timeline – have a far greater chance for success than those who do not. As an example, we shall consider the budget process from the perspective of the position I occupied for over a decade, the Naval S&T Resource Sponsor, and use the federal Fiscal Year 2015 program execution (October 1, 2014 – September 30, 2015) as the baseline (Note: My position was in the chain-of-command of the CNO. The function is performed today by the staff of the Chief of Naval Research, but the timelines are driven by Congress and have not changed.). The Resource Sponsor is the owner and defender of the budget, and must deal in parallel with three separate budgets (in execution, in Congress and in planning). As we shall see, the degree of influence that the Resource Sponsor (or any responsible individual or organization) may exert over program decisions depends entirely upon the process timeline.

The process of building the DOD FY-2015 budget began two years earlier, at the beginning of FY-2013 (October 2012). Within DOD, even budget development years were known until recently as POM (Program Objectives Memorandum) Years, and odd years were known as PR (Program Review) Years. In POM years, a six-year budget plan was developed, while the following PR years were intended to refine and make necessary adjustments for the remaining five years of the same period. This system was designed to accommodate past Congressional direction to focus on two-year budget cycles. In reality, Congress has always chosen to address each budget year independently, thus there was essentially no difference in the internal POM or PR processes. Beginning with FY-13, DOD dropped the PR Year designation entirely.

In the following discussion, we shall begin at the time of program execution and work back to the beginning of the process.

Execution Year (Dollars are appropriated, program is executed). Agency Program Managers own the decision.

Given that the respective Defense Authorization and Appropriation Acts are passed by Congress on schedule (a relatively rare event), execution of programs (the "E" of PPBE) begins in October of the execution year (for FY-15, this means October 1, 2014). The program managers are constrained by law to execute only the program of record, for which the formal documentation (Form R2 for DOD R&D) was prepared at least 15-18 months earlier. Execution must be consistent with the R2 descriptions as provided to and considered by Congress, meaning that there is very limited flexibility for program changes, and almost none for insertion of new initiatives. In almost all cases, new expenditures require dollar-for-dollar funding offsets. Reprogramming limits are very narrow, and, as we shall discuss later, all attempts to reprogram place existing funds at risk.

Within DOD, however, there is a small set of significant exceptions. The Assistant Secretary of Defense for Research and Engineering (ASDR&E) manages a handful of dedicated programs intended to select, fund and execute new programs within the execution year. These include initiatives such as the Small Business Innovation Research, Foreign Comparative Testing, Defense Acquisition Challenge and Quick Reaction Special Projects. These program opportunities are described on the ASDR&E and Advanced Systems and Concepts websites www.dod.mil/ddre/index.html; www. acq.osd.mil/asc). One other notable exception is sweep-up funding, which becomes available in the final quarter of each fiscal year. Programs that have not expended their dollars on schedule face the prospect of losing all unobligated funds after the end of June. The first objective of all agencies is to hold on to their money, i.e., obligate their dollars before they expire or are taken by someone else to pay other bills. Dropping off a compelling one-page proposal to an influential senior executive in the early summer occasionally pays off with an unexpected (albeit one-time) windfall.

Although the new fiscal year and program execution officially begins on 1 October, funding for Congressional earmarks normally will not be available for months, and sometimes years. Funds not included in a federal agency's PRESBUD submission may be rejected or even proposed as offsets to fund shortfalls of the receiving agency. At that point (with the few exceptions dependent upon the level of support for each earmark and the seniority of its supporter), Congress formally repeats its request to the agency to spend the money as directed in the Appropriation Bill. The agency, sometimes grudgingly, will begin the process for releasing earmarked dollars – usually starting slowly and only after all issues related to programs of higher interest to the agency are resolved. Other than those special interest programs of the most senior Members of Congress, the best case for release of earmarked dollars usually is March or April of the Execution Year. If a suitable contract vehicle is not already in place to facilitate movement of the earmarked dollars to the intended recipient, actual obligation of funds and contract execution may not occur for many more months. Federal regulations for competition and contracting are strict and fair by design, and government contracting officers (who have a very limited business sense of humor) are highly unlikely to cut corners to expedite the issue of a contract. Small companies counting on congressionally earmarked funds, but with no government contract vehicles in place to facilitate short-term movement of those funds, should plan conservatively, i.e., they should expect to see their first federal dollar no earlier than the final quarter of the fiscal year, at best.

Budget Year, February – September (Within eight months of program execution). Congress owns the decision.

The President's State of the Union Address in January is followed by release of the PRESBUD, traditionally on the following Monday, and completing the "B" phase of PPBE. From this point forward, budgetary changes can be made only through Congressional action, either via a plus-up addition of dollars or an earmark within the existing PRESBUD request. The PRESBUD is the default official position of every federal employee, appointed or career, and every member of the military services. "I support the President's Budget" is the required mantra for every senior official to a member of Congress or the Congressional staff. It is always true, however, that some parts of the PRESBUD are supported more strongly than others. Senior bureaucrats and Congressional representatives execute a delicate annual ballet to ensure – ethically – that the addition of the requests of Congress for their constituents at best enhance the essential programs of the agency or at worst create the least possible damage or disruption.

The activities of Congress define the trade space of the lobbying world. Without an experienced "consultant," private sector companies looking for Congressional support have little chance of success. For those whose proposals are not included in the formally submitted President's Budget, winter and early spring of the Budget Year represent a closing window of opportunity to secure federal funding in the upcoming fiscal year. Lobbying visits with members and their staffs increase dramatically in intensity in January and February. A growing number of members of Congress have chosen not to participate, and earmarking techniques have become far less visible and more creative in recent years, but the fact is that every member is afforded the opportunity to submit requests for funding of projects not included in the PRESBUD. The timeline for constituents to submit inputs to their respective Congressional delegations for the request lists varies slightly, but the deadline usually falls in mid-to late-February. The members typically submit their requests in mid-March. The probability that a funding request will survive the journey all the way to final appropriation improves considerably when it is supported by multiple members. The odds also improve significantly with the seniority of the requestors.

Defense programs, as we shall discuss later, must pass through Authorization Committees [House and Senate Armed Services Committees (HASC and SASC)] that establish policy and Appropriation Committees [House and Senate Appropriation Committees (HAC and SAC)] that provide the funding. The Defense Authorization Conference (harmonizing HASC and SASC issues) typically completes in June or July, and the Defense Appropriation Conference (harmonizing HAC and SAC Defense Subcommittee issues) in the August-September timeframe. When Congressional earmarks are appropriated but are not included in the Defense Authorization, they must be reconsidered and approved by the authorizing committees before dollars can be spent. Authorization of these projects often is a routine exercise, although positive results are not guaranteed. At the very least, the process is delayed significantly.

Budget Year, December and January (9-10 months before program execution). OMB owns the decision.

Prior to release of the President's Budget Request, the Office of Management and Budget (OMB) has the difficult and unenviable task of balancing the budget requests of every federal department (State, Defense, Commerce, Homeland Security, etc.), absorbing additional budget requests of the Administration and preparing the final PRESBUD in time to be discussed in the State of the Union Address. This means that department budgets must be released to OMB by late November or early December to allow sufficient time for the tradeoffs to be made. The most savvy senior bureaucrats make a point of being in the office between Christmas and New Year's Day This is because he most painful reductions are executed when the greatest number of department representatives are on leave for the holidays, thus are not available challenge the reductions.

Note: The following budget development discussions will focus specifically within DOD, then within the Department of Navy. Any federal agency with a formal budget development process, however, is constrained to a similar timeline because of the Congressional appropriation process. Agency processes are driven also by the number of Congressional oversight committees to which they must report. For any bureaucrat, fewer committees are better. DOD reports to four major committees (HASC, SASC, HAC and SAC), and other agencies (e.g., DHS) may answer to as many as a dozen.

Budget Year, October and November (11-12 months before program execution). The Secretary of Defense (DOD Comptroller) owns the decision.

Prior to release of a proposed Defense Budget to the OMB in December, the DOD Comptroller must balance the budget requests of the military services and Defense Agencies, incorporating numerous unfunded budget requirement requests of the office of the Secretary of Defense. Just as savvy Resource Sponsors ensure that their offices are manned during the week after Christmas, they do the same for "Black Friday." Many that choose to spend the day after Thanksgiving enjoying a four-day weekend return on Monday only to discover that millions of their precious program dollars somehow vanished over the extended holiday.

POM Year, July – September (13-15 months before program execution). The Secretary of the Navy (Comptroller) owns the decision.

Prior to release of the final proposed Department of Navy (DON) Budget to the DOD Comptroller in late September, the Navy Comptroller must balance the budget requests of the various commands of the Navy, as well as integrating the Marine Corps budget, incorporating unfunded budget requirement requests of the office of the Secretary of Defense (the second "P" in PPBE). During this period, the funding requirements are guaranteed to far exceed the dollars available, and the Navy Comptroller's final product is near-certain to leave everyone, and especially the S&T community (usually the Comptroller's first target for reductions), unhappy.

The final hours before budget release to DOD (and loss of DON control) can be very hectic, or worse. I still recall vividly a phone call from the Navy Comptroller at 4:30 PM on a September day to discuss the DON budget, which was many billions of dollars out of balance and required to be released at noon on the next day. The Secretary had just accepted a budget alternative that assigned half the overall reduction to Naval Science and Technology funding and spread the remainder across other Naval accounts. For Naval S&T, this meant an across-the board reduction of almost 30 percent for an account consisting of more than 5,000 projects. I immediately called the Technical Director of the Office of Naval Research to invite him to share in what was certain to be a highly traumatic process. Over a four-hour period, the two of us executed several billion dollars worth of program surgery, including our first-ever reduction (although less than half of fair-share) to the small but highly effective Marine Corps S&T Program. Countless hours were spent over the following months and years attempting to assess, and, as much as possible, to repair the damage.

POM Year, May – June (16-17 months before program execution). CNO (Director of Plans and Programs) owns the decision.

Prior to release of the proposed budget to the Navy Comptroller in July, the Director of Plans and Programs (and his/her Marine counterpart) must balance the Navy and Marine Corps operational requirements and budget requests of the various Office of the Chief of Naval Operations (OPNAV) and Marine Corps Resource Sponsors. During this period, the supporting program documents (Form R2s) are prepared by the individual Resource Sponsors. These R2s will be examined carefully in each succeeding review (Navy Comptroller, DOD Comptroller, OMB and Congress). Very important to understand: The R2s serve not only as justification for every DOD project, they also define what and how the program will be executed almost two years in the future. Program efforts in execution must be consistent with, and within the limits of the R2s as provided to the Congress.

POM Year, February – April (18-20 months before program execution). The S&T Resource Sponsor owns the decision.

Before the end of January, the Chief of Naval Research and each of the Naval Systems Commands must submit their requests for new starts, in priority order, to the Resource Sponsor. The process requires an offset (funding source) to be provided to pay for the requested new initiative. In a typical year, the list of program requests would exceed a thousand, but those for which offsets actually were offered usually could be counted on two hands or less. For the remaining 99.5 percent of requests, the words "deferred to the Resource Sponsor" usually appeared in the offset block. As the S&T Resource and Requirements Sponsor, my staff and I would dedicate the month of February and at least half of March to consider the 1,000 or more competing requests for new program starts, knowing that project-level new starts would be no more than ten. As the very first step of the process, we would examine emerging new requirements, issues for which a tax of the remaining account might be necessary. An example was the decision in the early 1990s to increase dramatically Navy and Marine Corps Mine Countermeasures S&T investment in response to warfighting lessons learned in Desert Storm. A firm ground rule was that no program changes would ever be considered that did not in some way address a future capability requirement. "Science for science's sake" is not the mission of DOD agencies, and "science fair" projects, no matter how intellectually intriguing they may be, have zero chance in a survival-of-the-fittest budget process.

The top line of the budget for every year of the POM is a fixed number, and this number can be counted on to be smaller than the number projected a year earlier. The budget must be zero-sum, and every addition requires a corresponding subtraction. Thus, consideration always is given to the tiny number of requests for which the requestor has provided a funding offset, as this is always an indication of a truly serious request. By the latter part of March, significant program decisions are made. The next 4-6 weeks are spent preparing the justification for and the briefing materials to support the agreed-upon program. Thus the budget decisions for projects that will begin in the Execution Year are made 19-20 months earlier, over a period of six-weeks.

POM Year, December – January (21-23 months before program execution). ONR and the Naval Systems Commands own the decision.

In January of the POM year, all Naval recipients of S&T funding must submit their requests for new starts, in priority order, to the Resource Sponsor. This includes each of the Naval Systems Commands and the Office of Naval Research. Thus in December each Command will integrate their respective internal divisions' inputs into a single Command request.

POM Year, October – November (23-24 months before program execution). ONR and Naval Systems Command divisions and/or program offices own the decision.

The first two months of the POM year is used to consider proposal options at the program manager level, the same population that will control execution two years in the future (the sometimes silent first "P" in PPBE). The process has come full circle. For companies or federal laboratories seeking Naval S&T funding, this period – two years in advance – represents the only chance to be included on an activity's request list. This requires that discussions with that activity must begin no later than summer or fall for programs that will be executed two years or more in the future! The overall two-year budget development timeline, driven by the PRESBUD submission and the requirement for Congressional review of federal agencies and appropriation of their funds, will not change until and unless Congress changes the way it appropriates, and earmarks, federal agency funding.

To deal effectively within such a system, it is vital to recognize that no single entity controls all or even part of the funding decision for more than two or three months at a time, and to understand the windows of opportunity for insertion of new ideas or changes are extremely narrow. The message is clear. Strategic planning, two years and more advance, is required for consistent success in the federal R&D space!

BUREAUCRACY 601
INNER WORKINGS AND FUNDAMENTAL TRUTHS OF THE BUREAUCRACY (INCLUDING PERSONAL OPINIONS, ANECDOTES, LIES AND HALF-TRUTHS)

Decision-making in the Bureaucracy

In terms of decision-making and getting things done, the most efficient form of government is that of a wise, capable and selfless benevolent dictator. Such leaders make good decisions in short order, always doing "the right thing" in the interests of their people. Unfortunately, such leaders are not only exceptionally rare, but share a common human tendency to become progressively less benevolent and selfless over time.

To their everlasting credit, the founding fathers recognized this fundamental truth and established the concept of separation of powers to ensure that America would never again be subject to the capricious rule of a king. The existence of three branches of government, each with equal powers and different (frequently opposing) interests, creates the requirement for all to reach a common consensus before decisions can be made and the business of government can be conducted. The resulting structure defined the federal bureaucracy. Despite almost every citizen's personal anecdotes and assertions suggesting the contrary, the federal system is quite logical, relatively predictable and fiercely neutral.

The inherent characteristic of any bureaucracy is that of multiple decision-makers of relatively equal power, spread across multiple cultures, with multiple interests. In such a world, the simple default solution for any issue is to share pain and rewards equally to all member parties. This action requires little or no coordination, and no one can complain about being treated unfairly. Unfortunately, excellence and mediocrity are rewarded equally, and there is no intrinsic incentive to excel. Bureaucratic cultures that operate by the default decision model, and there are many, give meaning to the term "faceless bureaucrat."

In the world of systems analysis, game theory or economics, a Pareto Optimal solution is a situation in which no one can be made better off without making someone else worse off. Pareto Optimal solutions are extremely important in a bureaucracy, but are difficult to achieve and sustain. Broad consensus and ownership of the decision must be obtained across multiple and diverse cultures. Coordination must be scrupulously maintained on a near-constant basis. Decision-makers must be kept equally informed to ensure their understanding of relevant facts is the same (most easily done with all participants together, at the same time and place).

Because bureaucracies represent a constantly changing landscape, decision-makers must remain flexible to accommodate externally-induced changes in people and/or circumstances. Bureaucratic decisions, therefore, should be made as late in the process as possible, to eliminate the maximum number of external issues. That said, there always is a right time to make the decision. The bureaucratic cop-out of delay past that point is itself a decision, and usually a worse decision than any of the other potential alternatives. A "good news/bad news" characteristic of the system is that because of the constantly changing landscape, few bureaucratic decisions are truly final, nor should they be, i.e., the Pareto Optimal solution may be a moving target.

A key element in the federal world is to work hard to develop win-win solutions whenever possible. Win-neutral ("I win, you break even") outcomes are less desirable, and usually are more acceptable to seasoned bureaucrats, who will live to fight another day, than to military leaders or appointees, whose personal timelines are shorter. Win-lose solutions always are bad, and lose-lose alternatives, usually created by external events, are even worse. Within the federal system, one has to always keep in mind that any funding change within a two year window of program execution requires at least one loser.

In the fast-moving world of the Pentagon, there are many important decisions, all made within a highly compressed timeline. Issues that are debated for two weeks at a field activity or two days at another headquarters organization might be made in two minutes or less in the Pentagon. Decisions, therefore, always are made with incomplete information, and program titles become extremely important. Sometime the title is literally the only information available to a senior decision-maker for making an up-down program choice.

Visual cues and recognizable images are far better than words; and few words are far better than many. Below is an actual example. Figure 9 is a proposal slide requested to be presented by a potential DOD sponsor.

OPERATIONAL ISSUE

Force Protection: Reducing fossil fuel requirements for forward/remote operating bases reduces the number of fuel convoys per re-supply period, thereby reducing the risk to attack for our CSS personnel engaged in convoy duties. Reducing the number of convoys per re-supply period could result in a net decrease in resources supporting CSS AOR-wide.

Figure 9. Operational Issue Slide
Adapted and reprinted with permission from DDR&E

The story can be told much more quickly and completely in two simple pictures.

Figure 10. Pakistani Delivery Truck
Reprinted with permission from DDR&E

Figure 10 illustrates a Pakistani fuel delivery truck loaded with barrels of diesel fuel. 90 percent will be used to power diesel electric generators at the Forward Operating Base.

Figure 11. Supply Convoy in Afghanistan
Reprinted with permission from DDR&E

Figure 11 illustrates the vulnerability of the truck convoys required to resupply fuel to the forward base. The words of Figure 9 do not paint an effective mental picture of the issue, but two simple photos graphically illustrate the message that the most important cost of fuel for the military at the tip of the spear is paid not in dollars, but in blood! In this case, the photos were sufficient to make the case, and DOD began a JCTD program to make its Forward Operating Bases more energy secure.

Working Inside the Bureaucracy – Rules to Live By

As a senior executive with the responsibility of ensuring that a few billion dollars of the taxpayers' money were well spent, I developed over time a list of fundamental truths of the bureaucratic system, and a personal set of rules of the road for how not just to survive, but to thrive in the system. The initial set was written specifically from the inside perspective, for the public servant who owns or influences the decision as to how money will be spent. The second set applies to those outside who are seeking program approval and/or funding from the inside.

My senior staff included seasoned career civilians to the SES and GS-15 levels and military officers to the O-6 level, veterans who understood these bureaucratic truths intuitively. Also included, however, were a half dozen or more executive development personnel from the Naval Warfare Centers, a highly talented group of GS-14/15 level scientists and engineers with the potential to become future leaders. Senior headquarters assignments sometimes can be a bit overwhelming for new members of the Pentagon system. In addition, there is no end to the list of people inside and outside who are ready and willing to offer "helpful" advice. Thus a standard opening day internal rules-of-the-road speech had to be endured by each of the newly-arriving staff members.

The following is the listing of my personal set of rules to live by for thriving inside the bureaucracy, followed by a brief discussion of each. They are intentionally a bit more black-and-white than the real world will allow.

25 Commandments for Bureaucrats Working on the Inside

1. There is no new money; there are no new starts.
2. Satan and the Comptroller never sleep.
3. The multitude of Christmas cards is not a reflection of your charm and sparkling personality.
4. Comptroller or Congressional staff interest in your program is a very bad sign.
5. When you don't know what to do, don't do anything! Stop and think.
6. Pay very close attention to the law of unintended consequences.
7. What's true may not be the truth – and ground truth isn't.
8. Follow the money, but own the decision.
9. Your best funding offsets (and budget defenses) are supplied by others.
10. Work with gravity.
11. When a problem has no solution, manage the problem.
12. When a problem is too hard, expand the problem (Eisenhower).
13. Money in motion is money at risk.
14. Reductions are forever.
15. Gold watches are best saved for retirements.
16. Stealth technology applies equally well to aircraft, budgets and bureaucrats.
17. "A prophet is not without honor, save in his own country, and in his own house (Matt 13:57)."
18. If you don't want an answer, don't ask the question.
19. No comes easy; yes takes a while (Mackie).
20. The most important person may not have the best title, but will have the best network.
21. Unlike wine and cheese, bad news does not improve with age.
22. Keep options open as long as possible.
23. Dance with the one that brung ya.
24. Don't Assume; Check the Facts.
25. It's always on the record.

1. There is no new money; there are no new starts.
Major politically-driven budget initiatives tend to occur about once every couple of decades (New Deal and WWII buildup, Race to the Moon and the Great Society, Defense buildup and Star Wars, current Economic Stimulus and Health Care). Except for such events, the top line of the federal budget is locked for many years in advance. Any program designated as a new start must displace funding – dollar-for-dollar – already set aside to carry a different program forward.

Public announcement of a new start usually provides an early Christmas present to a comptroller, congressional staffer or anyone else looking for funds. Delaying the new start "for one year" provides a source of funding to pay today's bills with dollars set aside for a program that has yet to begin, thus is easy to delay – easy pickings for any skilled bureaucrat! Needless to say, the same logic will be applied next year, then the year after, and the "new start" remains forever two years away.

The program manager's countermeasure, however, is simple; there are numerous "program upgrades," but never any "new starts". An example of this rule in action is to examine the lifetime development of the Navy's Standard Missile, which entered service in the mid-1950s, and remains in frontline service today. The modern version may have a different guidance, fuze, warhead, propulsion and airframe, but it retains the most critical component – the program title! So long as the title remains in place, every new generation of the missile is a "pre-planned product improvement" rather than a new start, and the program funding remains safely intact. A comparison of the Navy's frontline F-18 fighter aircraft reveals a similar story between the original and current versions.

2. Satan and the Comptroller never sleep.
The first priority of a senior executive in control of funding is to protect the money, without which even the most elegant of program plans cannot be executed. Protecting the money also happens to be priorities two, three, four and five. At some point, arguably somewhere between numbers six and ten, the next priority appears

– to spend the money in the most effective way. Thus the most effective senior bureaucrats spend a large amount of their time gathering and protecting the funding necessary to accomplish the highest priority missions. In the case of S&T, the ultimate benefits will not be realized until many years in the future, making S&T the "softest" of targets for those looking for dollars in the present. Enter the Comptroller, the great nemesis of the S&T advocate.

The first priority of the comptroller is to protect the agency's money, but from the nearer-term perspective of bills that must be paid today. This sly genius is far less concerned about the elegant technology widget that *may* save lives and dollars in ten years, than the fuel, body armor and other supplies that *will* save lives today. Although the comptroller's perspective is entirely appropriate, it guarantees that the "blue-sky tekkies" and the "bean counters" will be eternally at odds with each other. As a career technologist, I can testify under oath that there is no end to the schemes of the comptroller to separate the tekkie from his/her money. Examples are legion, but we shall consider three of the most notorious: (1) the Top Ten Technologies List; (2) the Bottom 10 percent List; and (3) the Black Friday Scam.

The Top Ten Technologies List
This scheme tends to appear with almost every change in administration, when a new set of rascals has come on board to cleanse the sins of the previous set of rascals. The scam begins with what appears to be an entirely reasonable request: Identify the agency's top ten technologies, to ensure that the most important technology initiatives are protected, and possibly accelerated. Once such a list is produced, four entirely predictable things happen, in sequential order. First, the comptroller looks at everything not on the list as "lower priority," thus as fair game for budget reductions. Second, the comptroller action is followed quickly by panic-speed requests to expand the Top Ten List, as someone's very important programs now have been identified and targeted for reduction. Third, the list expands as a number of important programs requiring protection are added. Fourth, the list eventually is discarded as its number of protected programs approaches the total number of projects in the

account. If my recollection is accurate, the last Top Ten List with which I was involved was discarded when the number exceeded 40. For managers caught in this scam, the order of the day is to insert every delaying tactic possible in releasing the initial list, make the list as long as possible, then to stonewall as much as possible until reason prevails and the list collapses under its own weight.

The Bottom 10 percent List
This scam is similar to the Top Ten List, but it appears much more frequently, and in many manifestations. The most straightforward approach is for the comptroller to request the lowest 10 percent priority for every account. Because all programs so identified become immediate funding offsets for the next unprogrammed funding requirement, the skilled bureaucrat will provide a defensive response something like: "Because R&D priorities vary with external requirements as well as constantly changing technological maturity and risk, such a list can be provided only at specific times and to support specifically identified unfunded requirements. Otherwise, such a list will become obsolete in very short order."

Because the comptroller also is a skilled bureaucrat and a worthy adversary, the attack is more often disguised, initiated through the highly dreaded "what-if" drill. A potential funding requirement is identified, and unlucky resource sponsors are asked to identify specific offsets to contribute their share of the bill. The safest response to such a request is to offer offsets most closely related to the funding requirement, e.g., a request for funds for jet fuel would lead to a corresponding aviation-related offset. With this approach, the comptroller cannot be certain that the offset represents your lowest overall priority. It also has the advantage of taking the money of the senior person in charge of aircraft technology, who, in all probability, created the initial funding request in the hope of spending your money rather than his/hers to cover an unwelcome unexpected bill. Best case, the offset drill remains only a drill and disappears with little or no damage. At worst, the beneficiaries of the funding pay their own bill, albeit indirectly, and the comptroller receives minimal actionable information concerning the program as a whole. A novice bureaucrat, however, may accept the "what-if" drill at face value and identify the overall lowest priority program as the offset. When this occurs, the comptroller has just been presented a precious gift, a package that either can be opened immediately or filed away for the next unexpected bill. Either way, the money is gone.

The Black Friday Scam
Although few seasoned bureaucrats will admit it publicly, we realize that the comptroller does operate under an honor code, even though it may be very different from our own. An unwritten rule within that code is that every hapless victim of a comptroller attack, no matter how vicious, is given an opportunity to defend his/her program before the money actually is taken. This is interpreted to mean that one phone call is made to inform the victim that his/her funds are in jeopardy and to offer an opportunity for the victim to provide a rationale as to why the dollars should come from the fraud, waste and abuse practiced by other program managers rather than from the exquisitely-crafted program currently under attack. Using the comptroller's twisted logic, should the manager(s) in question not care enough to be available at the time of the unexpected single call to defend their programs, the programs clearly were of lesser value. Thus the Black Friday Scam (Massacre?).

The day after Thanksgiving, "Black Friday" to retailers, is not a federal holiday, but the traditional door buster sales and the promise of a four-day weekend lure most federal employees to take that day as annual leave; most federal offices resemble ghost towns. The comptroller staff, however, is hard at work, having saved up a list of phone calls for the most heinous program reductions. If no one answers, the dollars have disappeared by the time the unfortunate program manager returns on Monday morning.

On Black Friday, my budget director and I would leave no phone unattended from 7 AM to 7 PM. Virtually every call that day would be from the comptroller staff. Once the caller realized that a live person was available to protest the proposed program cuts, the call would be terminated quickly to move on to the next victim, who was certain to have a very bad Monday morning in store. In like fashion, the most painful program cuts by agency headquarters or the Office of Management and Budget (OMB) tend to be made during the period between Christmas and New Year's Day, when the majority of federal workers are on leave.

Lest the reader conclude that only comptrollers use this evil practice, let us consider the essentially identical strategy of the White House, known as the "Recess Appointment." When a senior political appointment is too controversial for its confirmation by the Senate to be assured, the President also makes the appointment between Christmas and New Year's Day, when the Senate normally is in recess (e.g., the Bolton nomination as UN Ambassador). The Senate countermeasure is identical to the bureaucrat's tactic of staying by the phone; the Senate remains in session, even though only a single Senator may be present.

3. The multitude of Christmas cards is not a reflection of your charm and sparkling personality.
True public service should be a high calling, and it is vital that senior public servants maintain a sense of altruism and perspective with respect to their own importance and the importance of their position. An excellent example is that of President Harry Truman, a very senior leader who never took himself too seriously. Truman appreciated better than most the difference between the president as an individual and the presidency as an institution.

For senior federal bureaucrats, good looks and boyish/girlish charm may be wonderful assets, but potential influence over how a few billion dollars of federal funds are spent tends to carry quite a bit more weight on the outside. After one's position of influence is vacated, the number of cards, friendly calls and casual visits tends to decrease dramatically. Those cards that continue to arrive provide a good yardstick for calibration of the true friends. Those are the names that should remain indefinitely in the personal Rolodex.

4. Comptroller or Congressional staff interest in your program is a very bad sign.

Seasoned bureaucrats understand that Congress must approve programs at a highly-aggregated level (many millions to billions of dollars) because there simply is no time to do otherwise. Thus a question about a specific program almost never represents a thirst for knowledge of the questioner, but instead is a signal that your great idea has been identified as a candidate for reduction – to provide funds for someone else's great idea. Congressional committee professional staffers are experts at asking leading questions to facilitate a desired answer, and unsolicited inquiries from the Hill should never be assumed to be innocent.

On the other hand, scientists and engineers rank among the most innocent and gullible people on the planet, frequently with IQ and common sense inversely proportional to each other. We are eager to describe our work in the most minute detail to anyone who appears to express even the smallest shred of interest. We tend to be arrogantly optimistic, believing not only that we are unlocking the secrets of the universe, but that every citizen of the universe would share our passion if they only could understand the scientific elegance of our effort. Never mind that this is hogwash; most of us choose to believe it, nonetheless. It is for this reason that Congressional staffers and comptroller staffs – twins with bills to pay and always on the lookout for dollars – find easy pickings through their innocent-sounding requests for information.

Bottom line: Report Congressional inquiries – high or low level – to the appropriate office immediately. In most agencies there is a Congressional Affairs Director designated as the formal point of contact for Congressional communication. There also is usually a single individual designated, sometimes informally, for each category of inquiry. Anyone receiving a Congressional request should run, not walk, to that office and conduct all communication through their designated process and contacts. It is vital that the federal agency speak to Congress with a single voice. To do otherwise costs dollars, and, in some cases, careers. Because there is no new money, every increase in one program requires a corresponding reduction, usually within the same component of the agency.

That is not to imply that I did not speak frequently- on and off the record- to senior staffers and to members of Congress, many of whom became good friends over time. However, all congressional contacts were made – with zero exceptions – with full understanding of DON policy and with the knowledge and blessing of Naval Senior leadership, usually the Vice Chief of Naval Operations (VCNO) and the Assistant Secretary of the Navy for Research, Development and Acquisition [ASN(RD&A)]. Informal contacts made by anyone without appropriate authority are likely to ultimately result in funding or policy issues, sometimes without the knowledge of the guilty party.

5. When you don't know what to do, don't do anything. Stop and think.
I recall a minister's sermon from many decades ago on this subject, and his example has remained fresh over the years. I cannot verify the accuracy of the story, but in the words of the late Ron Vaughn, a wise federal executive and longtime friend, "If it didn't happen this way, it should have!"

The story concerns a WWII fighter pilot who once had been given the very good advice: "When you don't know what to do, don't do anything! Stop and think!" The pilot later found himself strafing an enemy airfield when an enemy shell exploded very near his aircraft. The pilot, dazed and disoriented, had the instant urge to pull back on the stick and to climb as quickly as possible out of harm's way. He remembered, however, the advice, and took a second or two to think before reacting. As his senses began to clear, he realized that that the fighter was streaking across the field very low, very fast – and inverted! The blast had blown the fighter upside-down, and the pilot's initial reaction to pull back on the stick and "climb" to safety would have cost him his life. In this case, the lifesaving strategy was the exact opposite.

Most "emergencies" in bureaucracies turn out to be false alarms, often no more than overreaction to an important person asking an innocent question. Mid-level bureaucrats, especially those who are less-talented and more insecure, seem to place a great deal of importance on the need to react immediately to every outside stimulus. This tendency is most apparent in political and military bureaucracies, where the appearance of action is important, even when the motion is essentially random. Reactive responses can lead to catastrophic results when a thoughtful response – and sometimes even an occasional non-response – to the same stimulus might resolve the perceived issue in short order. For the best bureaucrats, Rule 1 in an apparent emergency is: "Think first, and then react."

6. *Pay very close attention to the law of unintended consequences.*
Sir Isaac Newton postulated that "every action has an equal and opposite reaction." This law is not only basic in physics, but in life – and especially in a bureaucracy. One of the most dangerous bureaucratic actions is to establish policy that reacts to short term imperatives, often political, without adequate assessment of the potential long term consequences. Bureaucratic institutions can be intensely personality-dependent, and damage is especially severe when bad decisions lead to an unintended long term change in the character of the workforce a decade or more later. Most senior bureaucrats can provide enough examples to fill the Library of Congress.

Two good examples and their impacts are discussed in the Bureaucracy 401 chapter: (1) the change in the military double-dipping law and (2) the replacement of the Civil Service Retirement System (CSRS) by the less generous Federal Employee Retirement System (FERS). These combined synergistically to reduce cultural diversity in the federal executive mix – so useful in making informed decisions.

The negative technical consequences of the "Peace Dividend" decision in the early 1990s to downsize the federal civilian infrastructure are discussed in the Bureaucracy 301 Chapter. The budgetary impacts are much less visible, but are also highly significant. Ironically, the downsizing decision, made to reduce near-term costs, actually raised costs in both the near and long term. In essence, federal employees eligible to retire were offered a $25,000 buyout to leave federal service. The immediate effect was that employees already considering retirement accepted the windfall and left – the intended consequence. Bear in mind, however, that a senior federal employee making $100,000 would be paid on the order of $70,000 in the retirement pension. Thus the maximum savings to the taxpayer would be $30,000, and these savings accrue only if the position is eliminated and the work is no longer performed. More often than not, the job requirements remained, leading to one of two alternatives: (1) refilling with a less experienced person and paying the $100,000 salary *in addition to* the $70,000 retirement pay; or, (2) rehiring that same retiree as a contractor, with far higher than $100,000 salary and overhead, *in addition to* the $70K retirement pay. Also, the retiree as a contractor is unable by law to make certain financial decisions, putting additional work on someone else's plate.

As the White House displayed decreasing Civil Service workforce numbers, the numbers and costs of government contractors began to increase. In the following decade, there has arisen the entirely predictable outcry against the 1990s abrogation of federal responsibility and transfer of program decision authority to contractors, with consequent cost and schedule overruns. Likewise, there is the predictable push for increased federal presence in acquisition oversight. In the end, the federal downsizing decision produced short term political gains and long term cost and program quality consequences.

7. *What's true may not be the truth – and ground truth isn't.*
Anyone who has ever watched a political campaign – or watched the same news story reported on different networks – understands the difference between stating what is true and telling the truth.

Likewise, anyone who has served in an inherently personality-dependent bureaucracy knows that what is true in this instant may change in the next because of changes in people, policies or uncontrollable external events. The concept that ground truth may not exist or that it can become a moving target is difficult for many to grasp, but the federal bureaucracy has too many parts in constant motion to be completely defined or understood. A simple analogy is to determine the exact time – true for an instant, then changed by one, two, three seconds. Thus the statement of the time can be, at best, only approximately true. For better or worse, people, and policies will change. The most skilled bureaucrats recognize this fact, embrace it and take advantage of the inherent opportunities afforded by a system that is in a constant state of flux.

The old saying "figures lie and liars figure!" applies tenfold when one holds the purse strings for a few billion dollars that others would like to have. So how does a senior bureaucrat determine approximate ground truth? All too often, the answer is: "not very well." Within the public sector environment, the normal internal assumption is that issues will be presented in a neutral (i.e., most likely outcome) fashion, after active consideration of best and worst case scenarios. Thus, federal executives are far more likely than their private sector counterparts to accept proposal assertions at face value. On the other hand, presentations from the private sector, where loss of a contract translates into loss of jobs, tend to emphasize the best-case outcomes.

A personal observation is that neither side fully understands or appreciates the depth of this disconnect in perceptions, and that this misunderstanding is one of a number of reasons for the epidemic of cost and schedule overruns of the recent past. I frequently found myself frustrated when private sector executives applied "fudge-factors" to my assertions that were presented in the belief that they were as near ground truth as possible. My message to public sector executives is to expect outside proposals to represent highly optimistic outcomes and to ask hard questions before accepting proposal statements as fact. To the private sector, the message is that the public sector expects that you fully believe the proposed cost and schedule numbers, and that you will deliver 100 percent of the claims of your proposal as the most likely scenario.

8. Follow the money, but own the decision.
One of the first truisms most young federal employees hear is the "golden rule." Simply stated, "He who has the gold – rules" The Montgomery version is a bit different: "He who decides how the gold is distributed – rules" In fact, controlling the decision of how the gold is to be allocated without actually owning the gold can be the very best of all worlds. Examples are legion, but let us consider one from my own experience, recalling once again that "figures lie and liars figure."

The Bureaucracy 301 Chapter discusses how and why the "Peace Dividend" represented a severe blow to the DOD S&T accounts. Although they did not share in the Reagan Administration defense growth of the 1980s, they had to "pay their fair share" – and then some – in the downsizing years. Examination of the Naval S&T budget totals of the late 1990s, however, indicates a program that (in constant dollars) is relatively stable. In fact, the Navy had decreased the S&T budget by more than 10 percent, in direct noncompliance with the Office of the Secretary of Defense (OSD) stated policy of positive growth in the Service S&T accounts.

Resolution of the issue was an elegant piece of bureaucratic slight-of-hand, worthy of accolades. Rather than direct the Secretary of the Navy to follow guidance and to increase his S&T account total, the comptroller simply transferred to Navy the sponsorship of the four-star Joint Forces Command (JFCOM) Joint Experimentation Program (BA3 funding, which coincidentally happened to total about 10 percent of the size of the Naval S&T account). Voila: The Naval S&T account was now fully consistent with OSD guidance. All that was required was for the Secretary of the Navy to send a check each year to JFCOM and all would be well, at least in theory.

As the hapless Resource Sponsor, I had lost decision authority over 10 percent of the program, now controlled by a four-star general who was not likely to request my input for his budget allocation decisions. Far worse, the program funding total had grown by 10 percent, meaning that the numerous externally applied taxes were 10 percent higher. To add insult to injury, no taxes could be applied to the 10 percent portion of the program controlled by JFCOM. In effect, the Naval S&T account was subsidizing JFCOM by several millions of dollars each year. As the Resource Sponsor, I owned the money, but JFCOM owned the decision. The JFCOM program manager, on the other hand, was free not only from the daily drills inherent in managing a couple of hundred million dollars, but also from the requisite taxes that reduce the top line. And the reason was a budget game to demonstrate that Navy was compliant with guidance on S&T funding, i.e., to perpetuate the official party line. Note: This account does have a reasonably happy ending; sponsorship of JFCOM funding was eventually transferred back from Navy to DOD – where it receives appropriate scrutiny and must compete in the budget balancing and justification process.

9. *Your best funding offsets (and budget defenses) are supplied by others.*

Priority one for every Resource Sponsor (owner of money) must be to protect the dollars. As stated previously, it is also priorities two, three, four and five. At some point, spending the money in the best way begins to become important. Without funding, however, even the most important program will fail. This leads to one of the more painful tasks of senior civilians in the Pentagon – training insecure generals and admirals (usually newly promoted and/or new to the building) in the ways of protecting funds in the bureaucracy. Senior military officers don't particularly want to be trained by a civilian in the first place, especially when the lessons consist of showing why the military model under which they have spent the last quarter century may not work in the bureaucratic environment. Fortunately, the best senior officers "know what they don't know" and will listen, at least for a while, to the recommendations of a skilled senior executive.

On the other hand, no part of budget drill training is more frustrating to senior civilians than the first serious budget defense meeting of an insecure flag officer. The scenario follows a predictable course. The new leader begins with an internal senior staff meeting, explaining that the service had a critical shortfall, and that our organization set be a good example of sacrifice and offer our fair share, and possibly even more. The leader genuinely believes that such open support of the team also will stand him/her in good stead as a team player for the next round of promotions. On the contrary, this identifies to the world the presence of a bureaucratic neophyte. In the internal meeting, the staff pleas that every other person at the budget table will see this move as an incredible gift of dollars falls on deaf ears, and occasionally provokes a hostile response concerning loyalty, dedication and membership on Team America.

Budget drills are a daily occurrence in the federal system, and every Resource Sponsor is expected to be able to make the argument on a moment's notice that western civilization as we know it would be in extreme peril if said sponsor's budget decreased by even a single dollar – and heaven forbid a few million! In a true crisis, every real member of Team America will stand, deliver and sacrifice willingly. Unfortunately, what the new leader has yet to learn is that the overwhelming majority of bureaucratic budget drills are to pay for requirements that are of significantly lower priority than what is funded in the existing planned program. When this is true, and it usually is, sacrificing for the team means lowering the return on investment for the American taxpayer. Thus the correct opening statement must be "My program is far more important than either the proposed bill or the other potential offsets with which it could be paid." When the new requirement is truly of higher priority – as is sometimes the case – the truth quickly becomes apparent to all concerned. One fact is certain; every other veteran bureaucrat in the room will be opening a variant of the same script.

Because the script is common to all, the arguments of others on behalf of your money (as opposed to arguments protecting theirs) carry far more credibility than your own. An excellent technique for protecting money in a bureaucracy is to establish a role in which others come to you as their banker, investor and friend, i.e., you are holding in trust some of their money. Is follows the same fundamental bureaucratic principle of the requirement of broad ownership before a truly hard decision can be made. This is a difficult task; good senior executives will recognize immediately any shallow attempt to protect dollars. Those same executives, however, recognize sincerity, and a direct, honest approach usually will be successful. In any bureaucracy, the broader the base of support, the safer is the money!

10. Work with gravity.

Several years ago, a well-known four-star general gave me a terrific piece of advice: "It's good to be for what's going to happen." Many otherwise intelligent people waste countless hours, and sometimes careers, trying to push (or oppose) initiatives in an uphill battle when a far-simpler downhill approach is available and that is much more likely to succeed. Nowhere is this more apparent than in bureaucracies where long-established cultures exist, and where perturbations of those cultures are near-certain to face violent opposition. Within the federal bureaucracy, populated by appointee, military and career civilian cultures, an initiative that appeals especially strongly to one side may be a poison pill to one or both of the other two. Constant, open communication is the best approach, with every stakeholder included in and agreeing to the final answer. Because each culture is populated at senior levels by highly dedicated, intelligent professionals, a collaborative approach often produces also the best answer, not just the most acceptable compromise.

Coming to closure can be on occasion no more difficult than looking at the common facts from different perspectives. What appear to be a major change (e.g., transition from vinyl record albums to cassette tape to CDs and MP3s) frequently can be described either

(1) as a major industry paradigm shift, or (2) as a natural evolution of technology within an industry characterized by fundamental long term stability. The paradigm shift argument appeals to aggressive proponents of change, but alienates those more comfortable with the status quo. The evolution argument often is equally applicable, and appealing to everyone.

The agendas of political administrations overlay public policy actions, and often a specific politically-driven outcome appears to be inevitable. On those occasions when the expected outcome is seriously detrimental to the interests of the public, the best career public servants will choose to "lie down in front of the train," and do everything in their power to eliminate, or at least minimize the damage. Fortunately, more often than not the initiative will have enough good points that, with minor tweaking, it can be made at least acceptable, and sometimes even a good thing to do. In these cases, career public servants will work hand-in-hand with appointees – both sincerely wanting to "do the right thing" – to make the initiative the best it can be.

11. When a problem has no solution, manage the problem.
Scientists and engineers (S&Es) have been trained to expect that every problem, even a hard one, has a straightforward, albeit sometimes difficult, solution. We learn only later that all the problems with neat solutions were the ones included in our undergraduate and graduate textbooks. The rest of the problems, the ones without simple solutions, were waiting for us out in the real world. This is true whether solving an equation or resolving differences among diverse cultures.

The book of Genesis tells us that Abraham's sons Ishmael and Isaac traveled very different paths. Tensions between their descendents still exist, after thousands of years. Yet the simple fact that their descendents have multiplied and exist as nations today stands as testament to the fact that even problems that have proven unsolvable for generations do not have to be unmanageable. In the federal bureaucracy, unsolvable problems appear most often as mistakes of policy or action that cannot be changed at all, or that cannot be changed during the current political administration, mistakes that must be managed.

Watching a situation and consciously doing nothing is extremely difficult for problem-solving S&Es, but frequently can be the right decision for senior bureaucrats. Many unrelated pieces of a problem may be in motion simultaneously; letting some or all of these settle before acting is almost always a better idea than "just doing something." On the other hand, effective problem management may entail judicious application of pressure, just enough to maintain stability, for long periods of time. Learning to identify which problems can be managed but not resolved is a great challenge. For the novice, the imperative should be stop and think, then report concerns to superiors, realizing that he/she almost certainly does not understand the complete situation.

The superiors may employ the infamous bureaucratic management practice known as stonewalling, i.e., appearing to take action while actually attempting to maintain the status quo, and buying time to allow more favorable conditions to develop. Deliberate stonewalling is a dangerous practice, and should not be even considered except by the most skilled of bureaucrats – and then only when the executive is certain that he/she is fully informed on all facets of the issue. It is not uncommon for administration officials to expect (and sometimes desire) conscious stonewalling from the staff, providing "high cover" while necessary political promises are kept. The executive involved must understand the complete context, who made the "poor" decision and how and why it was made. Assuming the decision-maker was intelligent and reasonably well informed, the "poor" decision, once all the facts are understood, often is a far better choice that external appearances indicate.

12. When a problem is too hard, expand the problem (Eisenhower).

For many years I prided myself on creating a profound one-liner until learning that General, later President Dwight D. Eisenhower had the same thought a half-century or so earlier. Either way, the message is valid. When a problem looks too big and complex, often the best way to solve it is to back away and examine it from an even bigger picture. A good example is the issue of national energy security. When approached from the supply-centric standpoint of hydrocarbon fuels and other current energy sources, the problem appears almost insurmountable. From a broader perspective, when waste management and climate change issues are considered, their enabling solutions are synergistic with respect to conventional energy production, and the problem becomes far easier to solve – and with technologies than exist on the shelf today. The issues then become ones of public policy and political will, and not of technology, petroleum exploration or power lines.

13. Money in motion is money at risk.
Recall that the sponsor's priority is to protect the money. Recall also that the Comptroller is at the very least alleged to be a blood relative of Satan himself. Because of these financial tendencies, the Comptroller watches every reprogramming action carefully. Transactions below a set threshold are ignored, understood to be the requirements of doing business in a non-ideal world. Larger reprogramming actions, however, which require Comptroller (and sometimes Congressional) approval, stand out as if in a giant spotlight! The sponsor must request permission to transfer X million dollars from Program A to Program B. In doing so, by offering the reprogramming offset, the sponsor has just proceeded to identify Program A the lowest priority program in the account. The comptroller now has an opportunity to evaluate whether the sponsor's Program B is more or less important than the Comptroller's requirement to fund Program C, for which dollars have not yet been identified. Odds are very high that when to dust settles, the hapless sponsor will have lost the Program A dollars, and Program B is still unfunded.

14. Reductions are forever.
An age-old scam within the bureaucracy is the near-term budget or manpower cut in exchange for the promise of greater funds or a higher manpower ceiling the following cycle. It often is attempted with military officers who are in their first Pentagon tour and unfa-

miliar with civilian personnel practices and regulations (which are very different from military). In a four-decade career, I have not once seen this promise kept! Whether budget or manpower, the outyear levels are locked already at their highest possible values; they can only remain static at best or decrease in the future. If the resources are inadequate now, they are probable to be more inadequate in the future.

15. *Gold watches are best saved for retirements.*
In DOD budget terms, a gold watch is a program of very high value that has been disingenuously offered to be reduced, in the belief that it's clearly high value will protect it from reduction. To a seasoned bureaucrat, this provides great entertainment value as the reduction is graciously accepted and the unfortunate sponsor gasps for breath and, with eyes full of panic, wonders what to do next. Although examples inside the Pentagon are legendary, for any reasonably intelligent individual, only a single mistake is required for the lesson to be learned for a lifetime.

16. *Stealth technology applies equally well to aircraft, budgets and bureaucrats.*
The Naval Science and Technology budget for which this writer was responsible consisted of three accounts: Basic Research (BA1), Applied Research (BA2) and Advanced Technology Development (BA3). The primary objective as the Resource Sponsor was to protect the money, which meant creation of funding profiles as unremarkable as possible, not only for the S&T account as a whole, but also for each Budget Activity and for each Program Element within the Budget Activity.

Budget analysts search actively for funding profile discontinuities that indicate program starts or completions. As has been discussed earlier, new starts will be delayed (indefinitely), and the dollars swept to pay more immediate bills. Conversely, program completions indicate the presence of unprogrammed dollars in the future, and the amounts corresponding to the constant dollar value of the completed program are certain to disappear forever from the budget. The same argument applies also to program cancellations, except that current budget dollars may be lost in addition. Thus a sponsor will go to great lengths to ensure all funding profiles look as flat and bland as possible. Bottom line: In a budget of several hundred billion dollars, individual programs are at risk when attention is called to them. The most effective method of defense is invisibility.

Invisibility can be valuable for civil servants, also. Appointees and senior officers usually succeed through maintenance of a high-profile during their tour. For career public servants, your success means enabling their success. This may mean maintaining a deliberately low profile for credit or, conversely, a deliberately high profile for blame.

17. "A prophet is not without honor, save in his own country, and in his own house (Matt 13:57)."

These words, spoken by Jesus over 2,000 years ago, still apply equally well today. Our basic human nature is to discount the advice of those whose faults we know well, but readily accept the advice of others, of whose faults we are unaware. A primary message in my entry speech to the talented rising stars that came for 12 month assignments to learn the headquarters perspective was to expect frustration upon return to their home activity; their newfound knowledge and wisdom was certain to be discounted and unappreciated. Cultures simply don't appreciate being told when their perceptions are wrong, especially when the prophet is one of their own.

This provides an important lesson for each of us; we must recognize our inherent human tendency to filter opinions offered by those closest to us, even though they may provide the most accurate and objective source of information. In the workplace, constructive criticism is very difficult for a subordinate to deliver to a superior; neither side enjoys the experience. Because it is so difficult, when criticism is offered, listen very carefully!

18. If you don't want an answer, don't ask the question.

A weak leader asks permission before any controversial action; a strong one will recognize that sometimes to ask is to lose an opportunity. One of the most fascinating people of the 20th Century was Rear Admiral Grace Hopper, world famous as a pioneer in language development in the early days of the digital electronic computer. Admiral Hopper assembled around her a team of bright young professionals and let them innovate. Her famous quote "It's easier to ask forgiveness than it is to get permission" reveals a deep understanding of the federal bureaucracy, in which the concept of plausible deniability is essential for out-of-the-box innovation to occur.

Virtually every federal official desires deeply to do the right thing. Appointed and senior military officials, however, are more tightly constrained than career employees to support the formal positions of their chain-of-command. When asked a question formally, their answer must reflect the official position of the administration or Service they represent. On the other hand, when deliberately not asked formally, all want to see "the right thing" done for the American public.

This opens the door for arguably the most important unofficial duty of career senior civilians – to "do the right thing" while providing the necessary plausible deniability for superiors. This is not – repeat not – to imply that anyone should conduct operations without the knowledge of superiors, but rather to operate in a way that does not require the superior to make a decision that violates the standing policies or marching orders, even with the understanding that the decision is "the right thing".

A personal example: As the senior Naval career civilian for Science and Technology resources, one of the most important duties was to present and to justify the Navy and Marine Corps S&T Program to Congressional members and staff. In this role, only one time in my career did I visit Capitol Hill without including a counterpart senior executive from the Office of Naval Research. In this instance, my mission was to offer dollars from Basic

Research, a protected program in the Naval S&T account, as an offset to pay a bill to the House Appropriations Committee – in violation of formal policy of the Secretary of Defense. In this particular case, the same Basic Research dollars had already been removed from the budget by the Senate Appropriations Committee, with no chance of return. The choice became, in bridge-playing terms, either "to throw a loser on a loser," or to lose twice as much money; the sacred program dollars were lost in either event. Although I presented a personal, hand-written note detailing the Basic Research offset to the House Appropriations Committee staffer, every detail had been cleared in advance with appropriate officials – in a manner that plausible deniability was maintained for all concerned. Several days later, I was accused of acting dishonestly for execution of the funding decision by an individual unaware that all had been approved in advance by the person for whom he worked. Although not a pleasant experience, I must confess that I look back on the event with a touch of both pride and amusement.

19. No comes easy; yes takes a while (Mackie).
Walter H. "Tad" Mackie is one of the best civil servants with whom I have worked. Tad served for several years as the Naval S&T Budget Director, and also as my chief of staff. One day an excited Marine Colonel burst into his office with a "hair on fire" request for a budget reprogramming approval. He handed the document to Mr. Mackie, who began to read the request, and stood impatiently, waiting for a signature. After a few moments, he repeated again that an answer was required right away. Tad looked up and said, "All right, no!" He then said to the dumfounded Colonel "No comes easy; yes takes a while."

With these words, Mr. Mackie verbalized what should be an ironclad policy for all public servants, whether elected, appointed or career. Public service entails public trust, and with it comes the expectation that decisions affecting the public good will be made only after careful examination of the alternatives. Bismarck's famous "laws and sausages" quote implies that such careful examination frequently is not the case for lawmakers – but it should be.

20. The most important person may not have the best title, but will have the best network.
We have all met people to whom it's important for all to understand how very important they are. The irony is that they're likely to be people who aren't particularly important at all, and who contribute more than their share to the negative image of the bureaucrat. Insecure bureaucrats who are (on paper) the senior executives in charge usually surround themselves with large staffs, within which is almost always included a key individual who networks continuously, makes the system work and makes the insecure boss look good. Only a small amount of informal research, perhaps a phone call or two, is usually all that's required to identify "the man," who may be of any gender, size, color or title. This is the person with whom you must develop a trust relationship to be successful – although the titular boss may require occasional stroking. "The man" will be able to do with one phone call within his/her network what the boss won't be able to do at all without lots of staff help.

Accordingly, development of an effective network – the single most important bureaucratic asset – is essential for success in the system. For the fledgling bureaucrat, this means earning the respect and trust of people who can make things happen quickly when necessary, people who will need no more than your word to engage appropriately on the issue at hand. In this culture, your word must be your bond. One lie or deliberate half-truth, and you lose – permanently – the respect and support of the people without whom you cannot succeed!

21. Unlike wine and cheese, bad news does not improve with age.
In the Pentagon, decisions are made in seconds that might require days of deliberation elsewhere. The number of decisions and the lack of time to make them is not understood on the outside. When bad decisions are made or catastrophic events occur, it is critical that the information be passed – but only internally – to those affected. When learned quickly enough, the situation sometimes can be reversed. What not to do – ever – is to spread the bad news externally; the difficulty of external damage control completely overwhelms the ability to rectify the situation internally.

22. Keep options open as long as possible.

In a political campaign, the successful candidates scrupulously stay on message. In a military campaign, the General gives the order and the subordinates follow without hesitation to the best of their abilities. In a large bureaucracy, where decisions tend to be personality-dependent and many parts are in motion at all times, what is true in one instant of time may change in the next. On the day that these words are being written, two people with whom I have worked closely have announced significant new positions; a state official tapped to become a key White House advisor and a Congressional staffer moving to the private sector.

Constant change is the rule, not the exception, in the federal system, and strategies for working with the system must be highly adaptable to be successful. Whether selling to or making decisions within the bureaucracy, options should remain open until a decision is absolutely necessary. This rule tends to be intuitive with career civilians and appointees with politically-related backgrounds, but counter-intuitive to the culture and training of business executives and military leaders, for whom decisiveness and the ability to stay on course are justly admirable qualities. Unfortunately, in the federal system, they lead ultimately to failure.

Keeping options open, however, is very different from failure to make a decision – which is, in fact, a negative decision. At best, timing is perfect only once, and good executives recognize the right time and place, then act decisively. If marketing, it means to keep the elevator speech always on standby, ready to be delivered when the opportunity arises.

23. Dance with the one that brung ya.

When any official leaves their home organization for a temporary assignment in another, it is essential to remember that you are representing the positions and interests of the organization whose desk you are occupying. It was no secret that the Naval laboratories sent people to work on my staff to learn how to compete more effectively for dollars – which was entirely fair and appropriate. I tried to impress on each trainee, however, that there would be times that he/she would see information that would be inappropriate to pass to the home organization, at least not at that time, and that they would be trusted to do the right thing. I observed only one violation of that confidence, and it serves as a good case study of why the policy is in existence.

In the closing stages of the annual Naval S&T Budget development, my budget director and I were faced with a small end-game budget reduction. It was sufficiently small that we decided to apply it evenly to the entire account, with only the exception of the highest priority program, which we'll call Widget A, and which would be spared. In developing the budget, we conducted a purely artificial exercise in which the Widget A program was temporarily reduced to zero in the budget display, the remaining budget was taxed evenly, and then Widget A reinserted at its original value.

During the exercise, I printed for myself a paper copy of the resulting (artificial) budget to look over. The printer was in another room, and located not far from the desk of a person sent for a one-year assignment from the laboratory that led the Widget A Program. That person happened to notice the paper come out of the printer, and saw his laboratory's most important program apparently canceled! Instead of asking the budget director or me what was going on, he instead made a copy, then put the original sheet back in the printer. Minutes later, the copy was faxed to his laboratory Commander and Technical Director, then to the three-star Systems Commander, then to the four-star VCNO.

Within a half hour I was standing in the Vice Chief's office looking at a copy of the pilfered fax and explaining that not only had we not canceled the Widget A Program, but that in fact it was the only program in the entire Naval S&T Account that had been protected from reduction. At that point, the four-star VCNO personally dialed up the three-star Systems Commander and the O-6 Laboratory Commander, telling each in no uncertain terms to get their facts straight the next time before bringing false charges to his attention.

Neither the Budget Director nor I spoke to anyone of the incident, but word spread through the staff like wildfire. In demonstrating what he considered – honestly – to be his primary loyalty, the responsible individual's role as a member of the staff of the Chief of Naval Operations was diminished. Ironically, this also made it more difficult for the assignment to accomplish the goals of his parent organization.

Bottom line: It is vital to wear the hat of the organization in which you serve. If you can't do so in good conscience, move to another where you can.

24. Don't assume; Check the facts.
Bad assumptions and misunderstandings can lead to long term issues. In the mid 1990s I was having an intense budget discussion with another Naval senior executive, who commented that it was "common knowledge" that over the past five years I had significantly increased the S&T budget for my former laboratory (Naval Surface Warfare Center, Dahlgren Laboratory, which I left 15 years earlier). Upon hearing the allegation, I retrieved the data to show that the Dahlgren Laboratory's S&T budget actually had decreased, not increased, during the period. There was, however, a major increase in the budget for a different NSWC division to begin a specific program that addressed vital lessons learned in Desert Storm. In reality, every Naval laboratory, including Dahlgren, paid its fair share of the bill. The other executive had discovered a growth spike in the total NSWC budget, made an incorrect assumption of favoritism and distributed a marked-up NSWC budget slide within his organization to "prove" the existence of blatant favoritism. The false allegation never fully disappeared, and made subsequent activities with some members of the other organization unnecessarily difficult.

25. It's always on the record.
It is inevitable that statements made by those in authority will be repeated by others, sometimes incorrectly and far out of context. Most executives can list scores of personal examples. An especially frustrating case occurred for me personally in 2004 as

Executive Director of the Institute for Defense and Homeland Security. An IDHS program (still ongoing) was concerned with the monitoring of wildlife as carriers of potentially dangerous pathogens, whether natural or man-made. I referred frequently to the public information that a peregrine falcon carrying Avian Flu had been discovered in China, and that the birds are known to migrate from Asia to North America via the Pacific Flyway. One person with whom I had discussed the wildlife program (at the request of a Congressional staffer) stated the following day on a radio talk show that a peregrine falcon had been discovered in the US with Avian Flu but that the incident had not been made public by the Federal government. After the broadcast, I was identified to the interviewer as the source of the information. Needless to say, the following days were spent explaining to reporters that the suspect peregrine falcon indeed was discovered in Hong Kong, and not in North America, and that the event was entirely public information.

Marketing to the Bureaucracy – Rules to Live By

Except for those who have worked in senior headquarters assignments, most personnel inside the federal system are no better informed about how the system works than anyone else on the outside. The following rules for development and marketing of a program apply to all, public or private sector, who compete for federal funding.

12 Commandments – For Marketing to Federal Executives

1. "Keep up the great work!" means no!
2. Strategic planning starts at the back end, not at the beginning; focus on the final objective!
3. Tell the time; don't build the watch.
4. One man's pork is another man's bacon – both come from the same animal.
5. Federal executives accept plus-ups cautiously, but oppose earmarks vigorously!
6. Understand the culture.
7. Know what you don't know, and confirm what you do!
8. Complex equations have multiple solutions – yours is only one of many.
9. Authorization establishes policy; appropriation pays bills.
10. Cost avoidance is not synonymous with cost savings.
11. Persistence and dumb luck beat intelligence.
12. Final decisions aren't.

1. "Keep up the great work!" means no!

Of all the standard speeches given by senior bureaucrats, this is by far the most misunderstood. It represents also the primary exception to the usual tendency of career federal executives to present ground truth rather than optimism. The speech usually goes something like "This is an absolutely superb piece of work! We definitely will want to stay on top of what you're doing. Please keep me and my staff fully informed of your progress." When you hear these words, you have just been told no in the softest and most pleasant of ways – but no, nonetheless.

Most listeners, whether public or private sector, will choose to receive these words as "yes," even though an immediate positive answer normally will never be a possibility. Within the constraints of the federal budget, every unprogrammed dollar spent requires a one-for-one dollar offset.

The words will sound far less impressive to the untrained ear, but "maybe" represents a best case answer for a first encounter with a federal executive who has decision authority over funding. The "maybe" answer will sound something like "You have a promising proposal. I'll assign my staff to follow up with you to see if there's a possibility that it can be supported." While this will be received by some as lukewarm interest at best, the proposer has just been given good news. This is important to understand, so let's investigate further.

"Keep up the great work!" is a negative answer when spoken by a federal executive for two very good reasons. The first is cultural. Odds are high that none of us has ever told a houseguest "Your visit was a really stressful experience; please don't come to our home again!" We were far more likely to have said "Thanks so much for the lovely visit; let's do it again sometime!", then breathed a great sigh of relief as soon as the door was closed and remarked to our spouse some words about never making such a mistake again. Most civilized cultures are inherently polite, and most of us will go out of their way to be polite to guests. Sometimes this means saying words that are not entirely true, in an attempt to make everyone feel as comfortable as possible.

The second reason is more important, unique to the federal environment and usually not appreciated on the outside. Let's suppose Naval Senior Executive and S&T Resource Sponsor Montgomery remarks at the close of a presentation that the proposed technology solution for one reason or another will not receive further consideration for funding in the current budget cycle. The proponent of that technology, who has already invested a great deal of personal capital in the proposed effort and knows that failure to secure near-term federal funding is not an option, probably will conclude therefore that Montgomery does not possesses either the technical acumen or the mental capacity to appreciate the paradigm-breaking significance of the proposed effort.

With survival of the program (and possibly the company) at stake, the company president contacts the local member of Congress as quickly as possible to inform that an intransigent federal bureaucrat is blocking the path to national security, global energy independence, defeat of world hunger, a cure for cancer, etc. The member calls or writes the Secretary of the Navy to inform that a constituent has a program of special Congressional interest that is seriously underappreciated by the Secretary's S&T Resource Sponsor. A formal response to Congress now must be prepared for the Secretary's signature – ironically, by the same intransigent bureaucrat Montgomery. The memo will inform the member that either, (1) after further review, the proposal has been accepted for funding after all, or, (2) explains that although the proposal is a superb effort, possibly worthy of Nobel consideration, that resource limitations prevent its inclusion in the Naval S&T budget at the current time.

If Alternative #1 is chosen, an ongoing program must be decremented to pay the bill, and some unfortunate program manager is soon to receive an unexpected piece of bad news. If Alternative #2 is chosen (much more likely), upon receipt of the "Thank you for your interest in National Defense" letter, one of two things will happen. (1) The Member of Congress will decide that he/she has done his/her duty for the constituent and the case is closed. (2) The Naval S&T Appropriation will be earmarked in the upcoming year's budget to direct in law the funding of the constituent's program. For Montgomery, best case is that he wasted many valuable hours preparing formal responses, but the issue is resolved; worst case is that he wasted many hours preparing formal responses and now has a new bill to pay from within existing resources.

Let's return to the scene of the presentation, but assume this time Montgomery says to the speaker "This is an absolutely superb piece of work! We definitely will want to stay on top of what you're doing. Please keep me and my staff fully informed of your progress." It's no longer possible to make the case to the Congressman that an intransigent bureaucrat failed to appreciate the constituent's program. The Congressional letter to the Secretary is never written, no phone calls are made and the proposer keeps the Naval S&T staff informed on a regular basis as requested. The proposed program either disappears forever or competes again on a level playing field for funding in the next cycle, without Congressional special attention. Every seasoned federal executive will choose this alternative 100 percent of the time.

It is imperative to understand that this is not intended to be a message of despair to those who receive the "great work" speech. Senior executives see and make choices only among good alternatives; the bad ones are filtered out within the system far earlier. The time of a senior person is in extremely short supply, and the fact that you received time to make your case is in itself an indication that one or more staff members considered your proposal to be worthy. Always ask for staff feedback on how to improve the proposal, and stay in close touch. Persistence counts, and because the program almost certainly is worthy, it may well succeed on the second or third try. What is important is to recognize that the answer is no at the current time, and to plan future business decisions accordingly. Despite reputations to the contrary, few bureaucrats are truly intransigent, and, like almost everyone else in our society, we really enjoy saying yes and regret that we must say no so often, even when that is our job. With persistence, the answer next time may be yes.

2. Strategic planning starts at the back end, not at the beginning; focus on the final objective!

Yogi Berra, among others, is credited with making the statement "It's tough to make predictions, especially about the future." The strategic planner works not to predict, but to create a favorable future. This can be accomplished by beginning with a definition of the final objective, assessing neutrally the pros and cons of multiple approaches to accomplish the objective, and, keeping the end goal always in focus, remaining as flexible as possible in execution of the plan.

General McArthur's strategic plan for the defeat of Japan in WWII provides an excellent example. By mid-1942, the Japanese had established control of the island chains of the western and southwest Pacific. McArthur implemented a creative island-hopping strategy by which some of the most heavily-defended areas were bypassed in favor of more lightly defended areas farther up the "food chain." The strategy (1) arguably minimized Allied casualties; and (2) interrupted the logistics supply lines for the bypassed Japanese strongholds, and effectively removed them as a serious threat.

It is not the responsibility of the federal R&D executive across the table to support and further your superb technology, no matter how advanced it may be. It is his/her job to ensure sufficient capability of future systems and to maximize return on investment for the taxpayer. The federal acquisition manager will be far more impressed with a cradle-to-grave plan that includes a viable funding strategy than with a presentation of the most outstanding technology, especially when the presentation assumes inherently that if demonstrated, the technology is so outstanding that the government will have no choice but to buy it. The simple truth is that federal managers not only don't have to buy it, but if it doesn't fit within the approved acquisition budget – developed two years earlier – the law doesn't allow them to buy it!

For the technology developer on the outside, the objective must be the presence of your widget in a future federal procurement. To accomplish this goal, begin with the federal acquisition budget, which is available on-line. For DOD, the website is www.defenselink.mil/comptroller. Determine first the systems scheduled for acquisition over the next several years and then develop a viable strategy to dovetail your technology into the planned schedule. If your widget can't fit into an existing plan, success is highly unlikely. Small companies must keep in mind also the reality that ensuring the continued success of major US corporations and large systems integrators is essential (for economic, national security and political reasons); develop your strategies accordingly. When it's clear that "what's going to happen" is the introduction in five years of a military aircraft upgrade, then for any chance of success, your military aircraft widget development must be consistent with the established program budget and schedule.

The ever-present political realities of the expected procurement must also be recognized and taken into account. As evidence that political considerations can overlay even major military decisions, a neutral assessment of the McArthur island-hopping strategy discussed above must conclude that certain military actions were influenced by his personal agenda. The General's famous pronouncement "I shall return" upon leaving the Philippine Islands in 1942 guaranteed a future Pacific strategy that that included the invasion of Luzon, even if not necessarily the best decision from a military perspective.

3. Tell the time; don't build the watch.
One of the most common mistakes in marketing an R&D program to the federal government is for the speaker to spend lots of time to explaining the elegant technical details of the proposal. This is almost guaranteed to be a losing strategy. By the time it reaches senior levels, almost every proposal has passed through multiple common sense, laws of physics and technical quality filters; only good ideas make it to this point. As a result, technical excellence does not need to be proven; it is assumed. In the most successful presentations, the speaker spends far more time answering intelligent questions than describing program details.

The most common program presentations are allotted one half hour. My recommendations for creation of a 30 minute presentation follow:

General recommendations:
1. Plan to finish early. The session should go overtime only because the audience keeps asking questions (a very good sign), and never because the speaker has too much material (a very bad sign; often the kiss of death).
2. Allow an absolute minimum of 10 minutes for Q&A; 15 is better.
3. Except for the title, allow a maximum of two minutes for each presentation slide.
4. Plan to present 8-10 slides, with an absolute maximum of 12. Any additional information should be only in backup.
5. A slide should contain no more than five short bullets – and no complete sentences.
6. NEVER read the slides; amplify them. The audience can read as well as you.
7. Speak directly to the audience. If you can't, you're not sufficiently prepared.
8. Don't preach a sermon; invite a discussion.
9. If your case can't be made in 12 slides or less, your program has little chance of survival. Internally, the federal executive must be able to make your case in one or two sentences. Every good program, no matter how large, can be described in a one-liner, e.g., to develop the first atomic bomb, or to put a man on the moon and return him safely to earth before 1970.

Specific Recommendations for a Half Hour (10-12 Slides) Senior Executive Briefing:

Slide 1. Title
The title should be as short and as highly descriptive as possible. Let's create a hypothetical new proposed medical R&D program, based on successful Army and Naval synthetic hemoglobin work of the past. "SHARP (Synthetic Hemoglobin Advanced Research Program)" would be a catchy, but entirely nondescriptive title. "Synthetic Blood" would be far better. Very few senior executives

will ever know more about the program than its title, thus will have no understanding of the content or purpose, or even that it is a medical R&D program. "Synthetic Blood" is highly descriptive and creates a distinct mental picture. The presenter and proposed performers also should be identified on the title side. Plan to spend no more than 30 seconds with this slide on the screen.

Slide 2. Requirement/Problem Statement
What is the problem you're trying to address, stated from the perspective of the audience. Whenever possible, the requirement should be a "grabber" (e.g., a 40% or greater reduction in combat casualties, life cycle costs, fuel consumption, etc.). The requirement for "Synthetic Blood" might be to reduce combat deaths by 50% while reducing the logistics costs of hemoglobin storage and transport by 80% or more.

Slide 3. Program Objective
What will the program accomplish (e.g., development of synthetic blood up to the point where human trials can begin)?

Slide 4. Technical Approach
How will it be done (e.g., apply newly-emerging synthetic DNA technologies to synthetic blood products developed previously by Army and Navy to increase safety, increase storage life and reduce cost)?

Slide 5. Background
The past work that provides the technical foundation for the proposed effort.

Slides 6-9. Technical Plan and Deliverables
Specifically what will be done, how it will be done, who will do it and what will be the delivered product of the effort. Absolute maximum of four slides; two or three is better.

Slide 10. Program Cost and Schedule
What will be done, when and what is the final product? In simple terms.

Slide 11. Program Risk
What are the technical, schedule and cost risks? What is the backup plan?

Slide 12. Program Transition. Quo Vadis?
What is the way ahead for the program after completion of the proposed effort, what is the expected cost and who is paying for it? This may be the most difficult slide to complete, but a solid transition plan can be the best selling point for a program. It also helps the proposer to identify and build stakeholder support for the program by working with programs managers on the receiving end. Vague references to future capability improvements indicate to executives that little thought has been given to the transition, and can be a deal-breaker. Best case, the information on this slide is where the proposed effort actually began (solving a recognized problem) – and this slide finishes a complete story.

4. One man's pork is another man's bacon – both come from the same animal.
An interesting mental transformation occurs with members of Congress as the appropriation process moves forward. Most members sincerely want to "do the right thing," but realize quickly they can continue to do right things only if reelected. Reelection is made more secure when federal money appears in their respective states and Congressional districts. For many years, a pair of powerful senators inserted a $3 million earmark for a local research facility annually into the Naval Research Budget. Other than being the largest facility of its type, it essentially duplicated capabilities that were available a number of other places. Because the facility was paid for and grossly underutilized, I sent frequent letters to potential users, informing that it was available to them at essentially no cost. Takers, however, were very few.

While planning a business trip to the area, I decided that it might be worthwhile to check out the facility personally, and perhaps to formulate some new ideas as to how it could be put to better use. I purchased a local newspaper upon arrival in the city – a personal custom so as to be informed on issues of local interest.

The headline article almost leaped off the front page! There was a photo of the facility, its staff, local officials and glowing words of how the community was doing its part to enhance national security. The mini-epiphany hit me straight-on; the same program that was no more than pure pork to me was bacon to them – not only in jobs, but in honest civic pride! After returning to the Pentagon, I renewed my efforts as a federal senior executive to do my best to ensure that every federal dollar spent would have a positive return on investment for the American public. In this case, it meant spending more personal time with the senators' staffs on Capitol Hill and with the manager of the facility.

The lesson is an important one for the entrepreneur or community seeking Congressional funding. The federal executives on the inside are paid to maximize return on investment for the public. The effort as viewed through outside eyes may be essential to national security. Do not assume, however, that insiders will see or smell anything other than pork. You must make the case that convinces them otherwise. For transition of the technology to occur, all sides must believe in the product and work together to produce a win for the taxpayers.

5. Federal executives accept plus-ups cautiously, but oppose earmarks vigorously!

To most people, including those on Capitol Hill, plus-ups and earmarks are the same thing. To the federal manager, however, they are very different animals. The federal manager usually doesn't particularly enjoy Congressional help in managing his/her program. Unfortunately, Congress just happens to have a Constitutional oversight responsibility, and does enjoy exercising it.

Let us consider the federal manager responsible for the vital Red Widget Program, with a $10 million annual budget. Should Congress in its wisdom decide that the program also needs a $1 million green widget component, it can choose to add a $1 million plus-up with direction to spend the additional funds on green widgets, or it can earmark $1 million (within the $10 million budget total) for the same purpose. While usually not the preferred situation ($1 million bill still must be paid from somewhere on the inside), a plus-up allows the program manager to execute the Red Widget Program as planned, with the proviso that Company A in member B's district will also receive $1 million to develop green widgets – after Company A wins the requisite fair and open competition. In the best of worlds, the green widget addition actually enhances the program and the manager, taxpayers and Company A gain. Worst case, the money is not well spent and the program manager has an additional contract to manage. Either way, the plus-up usually does not disrupt program plans significantly – although the Red Widget manager and the agency may be offered the opportunity by Member B to absorb the green widget task in the next year's internal budget request.

A $1 million earmark within the same program is quite another matter. Now the best case is a $9 million Red Widget Program (10 percent reduction from the plan), the complication of an unprogrammed Congressional special interest task, and the probability of a similar action in the following year. For this reason, federal agencies can be expected to oppose uniformly any internal program earmarks. Most lobbyists will focus on directing funding to their clients, without regard to whether the dollars represent an earmark of existing funds or an additional plus-up over and above the planned program. Companies seeking Congressional funding need to understand that requests for plus-ups may not necessarily be perceived by federal managers as hostile actions, but earmarks (1) will be considered as hostile and (2) will be opposed vigorously on the inside.

6. Understand the culture.
When presenting a proposal to a federal decision-maker, the odds for success rise dramatically when the proposer understands the decision-maker's background and culture, whether political appointees, military or career civilian. Everyone loves to discover programs of low risk and high impact, but such opportunities appear only rarely. Most federal executives avoid high risk, with the occasional exception of emerging technologies that may have extremely high potential payoff. Appointees, whose tenure is the

shortest of the three, will tend to be most interested in proposals that (1) clearly support the administration's agenda, (2) can show near-term progress and (3) are technologically appealing. Depending on the timeline, risk can be less of an issue than with the other two cultures. Senior military leaders tend toward projects that (1) support military requirements and increase near-term capability, (2) have low schedule and budget risk and (3) can show distinct progress within a three year timeline. Senior career civilians are similar to military, but will accept a longer timeline, especially when the proposed programs dovetail seamlessly into the five year budget.

7. Know what you don't know, and confirm what you do!
Nothing destroys credibility more quickly than a person's making definitive statements to a listener who knows that the statements are incorrect. We all can name people for whom the most accurate description is "snake oil salesman," in its most negative, name-dropping connotation. Such people are the least likely of all to succeed with federal bureaucrats, who enter a majority of their conversations in the knowledge that the other person is considerably more interested in their federal dollars than in their personal charm.

A highly dramatic example occurred in my conference room during a proposal review. After the 20 minutes allocated to the presentation, I asked in the Q&A session that followed "Does the transition program manager (the person who must accept and pay for the future acquisition of the technology) support your proposal?" The answer was clear and definitive: "The program manager is Commander Smith, and he fully supports the proposal." From the back of the room, a voice called "I'm Commander Smith, and I've never heard of this program!" Needless to say, the presenter had a very bad day.

Most senior executives, public or private sector, become senior because they are able to recognize insincerity and separate truth from hyperbole. Unlike the private sector, however, the senior federal culture (especially when the culture includes military members) makes an initial assumption that statements or claims made in a discussion are, to the best knowledge of the speaker, ground truth. As a presenter from the outside, you normally will be granted the courtesy of this basic assumption of honesty. Most federal R&D executives are competent, well-educated and able to hold their own in technical discussions (although technical discussions usually are a very bad marketing strategy).

Some of the most painful mistakes of my career occurred when I believed that I understood ground truth on the subject at hand, but the person sitting across the table actually was more completely informed than I. Likewise, I have many times been on the receiving end of information that I knew to be totally incorrect. It is vital for each of us to recognize the point where our own in-depth knowledge breaks down and assumption or speculation begins. The experienced executive across the table may be far better informed than you, and credibility lost is almost impossible to retrieve. None of us have to know it all, and trying to demonstrate to others that we do is a losing strategy.

8. Complex equations have multiple solutions – yours is only one of many.

One would be hard-pressed to find any federal executive who did not believe they were doing their best, at least from their own perspective. One may disagree with their specific actions and decisions, but it is difficult to find fault with their motivations. Keep in mind that federal executives are paid to make difficult funding choices, usually among good alternatives.

Most entities or individuals marketing to the government begin with a specific technology – a single point solution – then attempt to convince the federal buyer that this solution is optimal for the problem at hand. This may be true, but it is likely also that competitors are presenting a similar message, all with their own respective solutions. Chances for success are far greater when marketers put themselves in the position of the decision-makers, who must remain focused on the requirement to be met, then attempt to choose the best among a number of acceptable alternatives. The best sales strategy is to show how the solution not only meets the requirement, but improves reliability, lowers life cycle costs and/or simplifies logistics, i.e., the solution that solves the most problems within budget constraints.

An excellent approach is to consider the problem from an entirely different direction, sometimes leading to an innovative, out of the box solution. This can be accomplished only when focused on the question rather than the answer, and can lead to an entirely new set of opportunities. My personal suggestion is to assign the problem to one or more very bright new members of your staff – the ones who have not yet learned why their ideas won't work. They may discover exciting to new ways to solve old problems.

9. *Authorization establishes policy; appropriation pays bills.*
I cannot recall a single year as a Resource Sponsor without at least one call from a contractor to inform me that the House and/or Senate Armed Services Committee (HASC and SASC) had approved millions of dollars for their program. My question in return was always the same: What is in the Appropriation? Frequently there would be silence on the other end, a silence reflecting a common misunderstanding of the fundamental differences between authorization and appropriation. Both are important, but serve different, and frequently misunderstood, functions.

The roles of authorization and appropriation can be understood easily with the analogy of a credit card account. Authorization is similar to the credit limit on the card. The card holder is allowed to make charges on the card, up to a preset limit. No money is provided to pay for the purchases, but the purchases up to the limit are *authorized*. The checking account used to pay the monthly credit card bill represents *appropriation*, i.e., dollars are available in hand to pay for the authorized charges. The Defense Authorization (HASC and SASC) gives DOD permission to establish a new office or to spend money on a program, but does not provide the dollars to do so. The Defense Appropriation (HAC and SAC) provides funding to execute the authorized projects.

There are every year a set of programs neither in the PRESBUD Request nor in the Defense Authorization Bill, but for which funds are added in the Defense Appropriation Bill. These "Appropriated, not Authorized" earmarks must be reconsidered and approved by the authorizing committees before dollars can be spent. Approval of these programs usually is likely, but is not guaranteed.

On the other hand, the reverse situation of "Authorized, but not Appropriated" almost never results in funds becoming available. Congress does not revisit the appropriation process, thus projects in this category can be executed only through internal adjustments. It is a rare case when a federal agency wants something badly enough to reprogram other dollars after Congressional appropriators have said no to the request.

10. Cost avoidance is not synonymous with cost savings.

My two daughters, blessed by an apparently limitless money supply otherwise known as mom and dad, spent much their teen years honing their power shopping skills to a fine art. Grown today, midway through their own federal careers and spending their own money, they have become much more accomplished at discerning the important difference between cost savings and cost avoidance. Many who market to the federal government either don't understand or choose to ignore that same difference. That ignorance is to their own detriment, for the federal executive surely knows.

Buying a car with the sunroof, metallic paint and pinstriping thrown in at no additional expense to you is cost avoidance. Buying the car with an unexpected $2000.00 factory rebate is cost savings – providing the purchase was a necessary and planned budget item. Federal managers are always on the lookout for true cost savings, techniques or technologies that, at the end of the day, lower a budgeted expense and free up additional dollars to apply elsewhere. Ideas that can be implemented within a two year budget timeline, are inexpensive to implement and save money quickly are very welcome in the federal space.

11. Persistence and dumb luck beat intelligence.

This is a good news – bad news story. The best idea may not win; bet instead on the most persistent idea. Most people over 40 are aware of the example of VHS vs. Beta formats for video recorders. The inherent two-year delay within the federal budget process, executed within a system in which administrations, appointees, military leaders and policies change on a regular, and arguably continuous, basis, leads to a situation in which opportunities for success and failure can appear again and again. Bad programs rarely get better over time, but good proposals that are well-received but fail in a first attempt frequently succeed in succeeding years. The key is for the proposer to take advantage of the next year getting to know potential supporters and to modify the proposal to support their needs. It is a certainty that friends of successful proposals and enemies of unsuccessful ones will change over time in the federal system. Whether selling a new program or holding on to an existing one, persistence is key.

12. Final decisions aren't.

Federal programs and policies are guaranteed to change, larger ones on cycles that mimic the tenures of the career senior civilians (roughly five years). Decisions change when people change, and what's up today probably will be down at some point in the future. Successful protection (and successful marketing) of programs therefore must be a never-ending exercise. Inherent with every senior personnel change is a requirement (and an opportunity) to educate a new individual and to gain or lose a friend, and an organization's support. Pouncing instantly on a new arrival isn't appreciated, but open the lines of communication relatively early and communicate often – provided the communication includes useful information. Communication for no other reason than to "stay on the radar screen" firmly establishes the communicator as having little of value to say, and in the end will do more harm than good. But when you don't like today's decision, just wait and stay alert. Chances are high that, given time, the unfavorable decision can be changed.

FINAL THOUGHTS

The best way to defeat an enemy is to make a friend.
The old saying that friends may be temporary, but enemies last forever contains more truth than most of us would like to believe. We can waste countless hours in real or imagined fights with those who disagree with us, compete with us, or just plain don't like the way we look! On the assumption that the perceived enemy is a loyal American, and one who does not come to the office scheming of ways to make things worse for the nation, there is hope. Even in situations where one person must win at expense of the other, the relationship need not be hostile. Senator and former Presidential candidate Bob Dole wisely described President Bill Clinton as his opponent, not his enemy. Some enemies always will remain, but trying to make friends is well worth the effort. When we do make the effort, it's amazing how often we learn that our perceptions of the "enemy" were wildly incorrect, and vice versa!

Making no enemies means making no difference
It is almost a certainty that bureaucrats with no enemies are the faceless bureaucrats that give the federal system a bad name. Anyone can blend in and disappear, and invisibility can be a great bureaucratic asset for the weak and strong alike. There are other times, however, that high visibility and strong leadership is required, and people of character will at those times rise to the occasion.

One committed person can make a big difference
History is filled with accounts of individuals willing to stand up for and act on their beliefs in the face of a determined establishment. Whether Columbus looking for a new world or Rickover developing a nuclear submarine, one person can make a difference. And the larger the bureaucracy, the greater the opportunity.

"Where there is no vision, the people perish (Proverbs 29:18)."
Our vision need not be profound, however. It only must be more acute than the vision of those surrounding, for, as Desiderius Erasmus observed five centuries ago –

"In the country of the blind, the one-eyed man is king!"

Finally, always remember to... *keep up the great work!*

APPENDIX A

History of the Department of Navy (DON) Warfare Center System

This report documents the history of the Naval warfare centers as a case study of the decline in in-house DOD S&T capability. Although the specific details vary somewhat, the concerns identified for the Naval activities apply equally to the other Service components of the DOD S&T enterprise. Thus it is logical to assume that many, if not all of the potential solutions for Department of Navy problems apply to all Services.

The evolution of the shore establishment and acquisition processes of the DON is characterized by 124 years of relative stability, followed by four decades of multiple, significant changes. The Naval Bureaus were established in 1842 as a replacement for the Board of Naval Commissioners, which provided management over Naval material affairs. After 124 years of survival through multiple wars and political administrations, the Bureaus were replaced in 1966 by six Systems Commands (SYSCOMS), which reported to the four-star Naval Material Command (NAVMAT).[19]

Under this new structure the SYSCOMS were charged with conceiving, developing, acquiring and logistically supporting Naval platforms and their weapons. This was accomplished through program offices, a field structure and industry, with technical support from Naval R&D activities (commanded by military officers but staffed predominantly by Civil Service employees) and university laboratories. The Director of Navy Laboratories (DNL) was established to provide representation, oversight and (loose) coordination of the Navy Laboratory and Warfare Center System. The university laboratories were placed administratively under the SYSCOMs for which they did the majority of work. The Naval R&D activities, however, although they received the majority of their funding from the SYSCOMs, reported administratively to NAVMAT and DNL, who was double-hatted also to the Assistant Secretary of the Navy for Research, Engineering and Systems.[20]

At the same time as NAVMAT was organizing, the Director, Defense Research and Engineering (DDR&E, Dr. John Foster) asked Dr. Leonard Sheingold, vice president of Sylvania Electronic Systems, to chair the Defense Science Board (DSB) Task Force on DOD In-House Laboratories. The Sheingold study proposed that individual laboratories be reorganized into technical centers, each possessing a "critical mass" of one thousand specialists performing R&D as well as demonstrating the workability of prototypes. About 70 percent of the effort would be devoted to in-house activities rather than contract monitoring, and each center director would control the resources necessary to accomplish the mission. Within days of the formal release of the Sheingold Report, DDR&E directed the Navy to initiate plans to establish weapon systems development centers.[21]

Timing was excellent for staffing of the Navy's new R&D centers. Science and Technology funding was at its all-time high, partially a result of the race into space and the national goal established by President Kennedy to put an American on the moon by the end of the decade. Added to those lofty and noble goals of national interests, space exploration, scientific discovery and contributing to the interests of one's country, employment by a military laboratory held the promise also of occupational draft deferments for a growing population of baby-boom male scientists and engineers (S&Es), many of whom did not relish the thought of being drafted into ground combat in the nation's most unpopular war. In addition, scientific employment opportunities took a drastic downturn at the end of the decade, and new M.S. and Ph.D. degree scientists offered to accept Civil Service employment at entry levels as low as GS-5 instead of the usual GS-9/11/12. Thus the DOD and Naval R&D establishment was able to increase its staff easily, picking and choosing from the most talented of young scientists and engineers. The centers also enhanced the education levels and kept morale high through formal professional training programs and graduate education, frequently provided on site.

The Naval Material Command proved to be a good steward of the Naval R&D centers for the nearly two decades of its existence. Even though S&T funding dropped sharply during the latter years of the Viet Nam War and declined at a pace of about two percent per year for the rest of the decade (and since), the Naval Laboratory and warfare center community and associated university labs developed and transitioned the requisite technologies for such advanced systems as the Aegis Combat System, towed arrays, GPS, laser-guided projectiles, reactive weapons, and directed energy technology, to name only a few.

However, life in the "DNL Labs," as the community was known, changed dramatically in April 1985 when Navy Secretary John Lehman announced the disestablishment of the Naval Material Command, beginning a period of instability in the Naval technical community that arguably continues to this day. The R&D centers and the university laboratory responsibilities were placed initially under the Office of Naval Research (ONR), but ONR was not prepared to manage such a large component (over twenty thousand people) of the shore establishment. Less than a year later they were moved to the Space and Naval Warfare Systems Command (SPAWAR), newly created to oversee systems architecture. Unfortunately for the warfare centers, laboratory management was not a vital interest of a command facing the difficult task of creating the Naval system for Warfare Systems Architecture and Engineering. Furthermore, SPAWAR was placed in the unenviable position of coordinating the activities of warfare centers that received most of their funding from other (peer, but larger) Systems Commands.[22]

The SPAWAR laboratory management era ended in January 1992 when the office of the Director of Navy Laboratories was formally abolished. Four new "megacenters" were established (Air, Command, Control and Ocean Surveillance, Surface, Undersea), with each center reporting to the SYSCOM representing its major source of income.[23] The movement of the warfare centers under the Naval Systems Commands was the most visible of three major events in the early 1990s that fundamentally changed the character of DON S&T execution. This move occurred despite deep concerns within the R&D community that the near-term focus necessary for the SYSCOMs to accomplish their primary missions would lead to a slow degradation of the long-term (S&T) capabilities of the warfare centers.

After the disestablishment of DNL, the Laboratory/Center oversight function was intended to be performed by two new committees. The Navy Laboratory and Center Oversight Committee (NLCOC), chaired by the Assistant Secretary of the Navy for Research, Development and Acquisition [ASN (RDA)] and including the Vice CNO and Assistant Commandant of the Marine Corps as principal members and Systems Commanders as associate members, was to provide policy level oversight. The last meeting of the NLCOC was in 1992. The Navy Laboratory/Center Coordinating Group (NLCCG), which includes the commanders and technical directors of the warfare centers and the Commanding Officer and Director of Research of NRL, has remained semi-active. This forum is effective as a vehicle for communication among the members of the community, but is designed to focus inward rather than on Naval policy and external representation issues.

A second event occurred almost unnoticed in 1991, but which had a significant effect on the national and Naval technology base. PL-914-41, Section 203, of the 1971 Military Personnel Authorization, provided for private industry recovery of Independent Research and Development (IR&D) expenses as general and administrative overhead, for building of the future business and technology base. Companies with IR&D programs in excess of $4 million were required (1) to submit a technical plan describing each technical project, which the DOD would evaluate for "potential military relationship;" (2) to negotiate an agreement with the DOD which established an IR&D ceiling for cost recovery (Note: Most companies exceeded the cost recovery ceiling each year, with company dollars paying as much as one-third of the total IR&D.); and (3) to present an on-site review of its IR&D program to the DOD at least once every three years.[24] In December 1991, responding to pressure from industry to simplify the process and to allow full recovery of IR&D expenses, Congress passed PL-102-190, which stated "that independent R&D and B&P costs of DOD contractors shall be allowable as indirect costs on covered contracts to the extent that such costs are allocable, reasonable, and not otherwise unallowable by law or under the Federal Acquisition (FAR)." The legislation allowed full recovery of IR&D expenses and negated the requirement for IR&D ceiling negotiations with DOD (industry's primary goal in pursuing the legislation) but also negated the requirement for industry reporting and DOD review and oversight of IR&D.[25]

From a national technology base perspective, PL-102-90 produced two highly negative unintended consequences. First, it allowed (thus effectively encouraged) industry to reduce overhead rates by reducing IR&D investment. IR&D budgets shrank almost instantly to less than half their levels before the law change, and the character of IR&D work became nearer-term (more like B&P funding) as the Reagan defense budget dropped to the Bush and Clinton administration levels. Second, the DOD and industry lost overnight a forcing function to encourage and assure access by individual performers to each other's R&D, ending a period of many years of mutually advantageous technical communication and leverage between the public and private sectors. Ironically, although demands for leverage of private sector technology increased steadily throughout the decade following passage of PL-102-90, private sector technology development became, with few exceptions, far less visible to the DOD.

The third event was the loss of the 6.2 Laboratory Independent Exploratory Development (IED) Program in 1993, canceled because of DON S&T reductions and a historically difficult Congressional budget defense (a casualty of Congressional staff concerns over after-the-fact program review and oversight). IED was a relatively small account (nominally $25 million/year), with funding allocated to NRL and the warfare centers to complement the 6.1 Laboratory Independent Research Program of similar size, which still exists today. These programs represented together an exceptionally effective DON investment in new, generally high-risk/high-payoff technologies – "disruptive technologies," in the terminology of Bower and Christenson[26], that has become a 21st century term of choice. IED funding at a specific Division site was modest (e.g., an activity the size of NSWC's Carderock Division might receive $2 million each of Independent Research and IED funds.) and frequently was divided into increments of less than one work-year each. Selection of projects for ILIR or IED funding gave NRL and the warfare centers an excellent way to reward innovation and to encourage the best and brightest. Technologies such as GPS, reactive weapons and submarine bow planes were supported in their infancy with IED funds. The loss of IED represented a major blow to the S&T communities within the centers, forcing many scientists and engineers into non-S&T career paths.

After the cancellation of IED, ONR created and maintained a similar Applied Research "Base Program" at the Naval Research Laboratory. The concept proved to be an important resource for the NRL Director of Research to assure future excellence in research and to reward innovation. Base Program funding has been Congressionally defensible (unlike IED, for which defense was difficult), but S&T base programs were not established at the four major warfare centers.

In 1995, the Naval Air Warfare Center headquarters staff was disestablished, and the R&D and S&T activities remaining from what was known in 1985 as the Naval Weapons Center and the Naval Air Development Center were integrated into the NAVAIR structure. Three years later the components of the DON C4I R&D infrastructure were integrated into SPAWAR. NAVSEA integrated the Naval Surface Warfare Center (NSWC) and Naval Undersea Warfare Center (NUWC) components into its structure in 1999, but both maintained individual warfare center identities and civilian Technical Director positions.

The Marine Corps became a new player within the DOD laboratory system in 1995 when the Commandant established the Marine Corps Warfighting Laboratory (MCWL) at Quantico, Virginia. Through a series of major exercises and warfighting experiments, MCWL introduced the first "Battle Lab" of the DON. In 2001,

MCWL established its first civilian Technical Director position, to make the organization more compatible with the Naval RDT&E infrastructure and to ensure corporate memory.

Thus the DON entered the new millennium with a SYSCOM-centric warfare center infrastructure and a new and growing Marine Corps R&D presence. The current organizational structure is arguably better coupled to the acquisition and budget processes than in the old "DNL Lab" days. There are potentially serious near and long-term issues, however, which include:

1. An aging senior work force, with an entire generation retired or retirement-eligible and potentially without trained replacements in the pipeline to carry forward;
2. A Naval S&T budget that has declined steadily since the 1960s, specifically in Applied Research;
3. Declining industry IR&D investment, focused primarily on the short-term since the early 1990s (not an alternative to DOD S&T);
4. The need for a strategic vision for the DON RDT&E infrastructure and resources to focus technology investment and assure technological superiority for the Navy-After-Next.

LIST OF ABBREVIATIONS

ACD&P	Advanced Component Development and Prototypes
ACTD	Advanced Concept Technology Demonstrations
AFOSR	Air Force Office of Scientific Research
AFRL	Air Force Research Laboratory
ARO	Army Research Office
ASN (RD&A)	Assistant Secretary of the Navy for Research, Development and Acquisition
ATD	Advanced Technology Demonstrations
B&P	Bid and Proposal
BA	Budget Activity
BMDO	Ballistic Missile Defense Office
BRL	Business Readiness Level
CNO	Chief of Naval Operations
CSRS	Civil Service Retirement System
DARPA	Defense Advanced Projects Research Agency
DDR&E	Director, Defense Research and Engineering
DHS	Department of Homeland Security
DNL	Director of Navy Laboratories
DOD	Department of Defense
DON	Department of Navy
DSB	Defense Science Board
FERS	Federal Employee Retirement System
FFRDC	Federally Funded Research and Development Centers
FY-13	Fiscal Year 2013
FYDP	Future Year Development Plan
GS	General Schedule
HAC	House Appropriations Committee
HASC	House Armed Services Committee
JROC	Joint Requirements Oversight Council
IDHS	Institute for Defense and Homeland Security
IED	Independent Exploratory Development
IOT&E	Initial Operational Test and Evaluation
IPA	Intergovernmental Personnel Act

IR&D	Independent Research and Development
JCTD	Joint Capability Technology Demonstrations
JFCOM	Joint Forces Command
MCWL	Marine Corps Warfighting Laboratory
MDA	Missile Defense Agency
MRL	Manufacturing Readiness Level
MANTECH	Manufacturing Technology
NAWC	Naval Air Warfare Center
NLCCG	Naval Laboratory and Center Coordinating Group
NLCOC	Naval Laboratory and Center Oversight Committee
NMC	Naval Material Command
NRL	Naval Research Laboratory
NSF	National Science Foundation
NSWC	Naval Surface Warfare Center
NUWC	Naval Undersea Warfare Center
OMB	Office of Management and Budget
ONR	Office of Naval Research
OPNAV	Office of the Chief of Naval Operations
OSD	Office of the Secretary Of Defense
PE	Program Element
POM	Program Objectives Memorandum
PPBE	Planning, Programming, Budgeting and Execution Process
PRESBUD	President's Budget
Q&A	Question and Answer
R&D	Research and Development
RDT&E	Research, Development, Test, and Evaluation
ROI	Return on Investment
S&E	Science and Engineering
S&Es	Scientists and Engineers
S&T	Science and Technology
SAC	Senate Appropriation Committee
SASC	Senate Armed Services Committee
SBIR	Small-Business Innovation Research
SYSCOMS	Systems Commands
SDI	Strategic Defense Initiative

SDIO	Strategic Defense Initiative Office
SES	Senior Executive Service
SPAWAR	Space and Naval Warfare Systems Command
SSC	SPAWAR Systems Center
TRL	Technology Readiness Level
UARC	University Affiliated Research Centers
UN	United Nations

REFERENCES

1. DOD Joint Concept Technology Demonstration website, http://www.acq.osd.mil/jctd/TRL.htm.
2. DOD Financial Management Regulation 7000.14-R – DOD Financial Management Regulation Volume 2B, Chapter 5.
3. Ibid.
4. Ibid.
5. Ibid.
6. Ibid.
7. Ibid.
8. Ibid.
9. Ibid.
10. "Report of the Defense Science Board Task Force on the Defense Industrial and Technology Base, Volume I/II (DTIC #ADA 202469 and #ADA 212698)," 1988.
11. Naval Advanced Technology Demonstration (ATD) Policy Instruction, June 1996.
12. Weinberger, Caspar W., "The R&D Key," *Defense* 83, February 1983, 2.
13. Roosevelt, Franklin D., Presidential letter to Dr. Vannevar Bush, Director of the Office of Scientific Research and Development, November 17, 1944.
14. Bush, Vannevar, Report to the President, "Science, the Endless Frontier," July, 1945.
15. Public Law PL-914-41, Section 203, 1971 DOD Military Procurement Authorization Act.
16. Public Law PL-102-190, Section 802, National Defense Authorization Act for Fiscal Years 1992 and 1993.
17. Caiden, Martin, Air Force; A Pictoral History of American Airpower, Bramhall House, 1957, 78.
18. Public Law PL-106-65, Section 651, National Defense Authorization Act for Fiscal Year 2000.
19. Colvard, James E., White paper, "Some thoughts on the Navy's organization Under the DMR," January 1992, 1-2.
20. Ibid. ref 2.
21. Carlisle, Rodney P., "Management of the U.S. Navy Research

and Development Centers During the Cold War," Navy Laboratory/Center Coordinating Group and Naval Historical Center Publication, 1996, 41-43.
22. Ibid, ref 19.
23. Ibid, ref 21.
24. Public Law PL-914-41, Section 203.
25. Public Law PL-102-190, Section 802.
26. Bower, Joseph L. and Christensen, Clayton M., "Disruptive Technologies: Catching the Wave," *Harvard Business Review*, January-February 1995, 43-53.

INDEX

12 Commandments ix, 127
25 Commandments viii, 100
600 Ship Navy 48

Abraham 115
academia 26, 44, 52
ACD&P 30, 31, 33, 38, 152
Acquisition vi, 21, 22, 27-30, 33, 35-38, 40, 50, 59, 61-64, 109, 131, 138, 145, 151
ACTD 36, 152
Admiral vi, ix, 71, 73, 120
Advanced Component Development and Prototypes. *See* ACD&P
Advanced Concept Technology Demonstrations. *See* ACTD
Advanced Systems and Concepts 36, 86
Advanced Technology Demonstrations. *See* ATDs
Aegis Combat System 147
AFOSR 21, 45, 152
AFRL 41, 152
aircraft 20, 31, 59, 73, 100, 101, 103, 107, 118, 132
Air Force 12, 21, 22, 41, 42, 45, 53, 59, 72, 152
Air Force Materiel Command 22, 41
Air Force Office of Scientific Research. *See* AFOSR
Air Force Research Laboratory. *See* AFRL
algorithms 36

America(n) 11, 30, 34, 44, 49, 51, 55, 57, 66, 68, 71, 73, 81, 84, 94, 113, 120, 126, 136, 143, 146
analytical studies 20
Applied Physics Laboratory 25
Applied Research 21, 23-26, 29, 32, 34, 41, 45, 46, 47, 48, 49, 51, 55, 57, 58, 61, 65, 118, 150, 151
Armed Services Committee 88, 140, 152, 153
Army 12, 21, 22, 37, 41, 42, 45, 59, 72, 73, 133, 134, 152
Army Research Office. *See* ARO
ARO 21, 45, 152
ATD 35, 36, 152
atomic bomb 133
Avian Flu 126

BA 22-24, 27, 28, 30-34, 36, 41, 47, 118, 152
Baciocco, Albert J. ix, x
Basic Research 21-26, 29, 30, 32, 34, 44, 45, 47, 61, 65, 118, 120, 121
Battle of Midway 59
Battle of the Atlantic 51
Berlin 54, 57
Berlin Wall 54
Bid-and-Proposal. *See* B&P
Black Friday 89, 102, 104
BMDO 39, 40, 152
Bower, Joseph L. 150
B&P 60, 61, 149, 152

breadboard 20, 24, 25
BRLs 19
Budget Activities. *See* BA
Budget Director 121, 125
bureaucracy vi, vii, viii, ix,
    11, 12, 13, 14, 35, 56, 66,
    69, 71, 74, 77, 94, 95, 99,
    108, 110, 112, 114, 115,
    117, 120, 123, 143
bureaucrat viii, 11, 77-80, 89,
    95, 100, 101, 103, 105, 110,
    113, 118, 122, 129, 130
Business Readiness Levels.
    See BRLs

Capitol Hill 83, 120, 136
Captain 12, 22, 42, 71, 75, 76
Carderock, MD 42, 150
Chief of Naval Operations
    125
Chief of Naval Research 59
Chiefs of Staff 40
China Lake 51
civilian 12, 14, 42, 57, 59, 67,
    68, 69, 75-77, 81, 112, 114,
    118, 120, 137, 150, 151
Civil Service 57, 59, 70, 74-
    77, 80-82, 108, 109, 145,
    146, 152
Civil Service Retirement
    System. *See* CSRS
Clinton, Bill 143
Colonel 12, 22, 71, 75, 76,
    121
Colvard, Dr. James 68
Commander 73, 124, 138
Commander-in-Chief 73
Commanding Officer 42, 148
Commandments vi
communications 23
Comptroller vi, 33, 89-91,
    100-103, 106, 111, 117

Congress 37, 49, 51, 55, 60,
    75, 79, 106-108, 129, 135,
    136, 141, 148
Congressional 14, 26, 37, 38,
    47, 49, 66, 68, 69, 84, 100,
    106, 117, 120, 123, 126,
    129, 130, 135, 136, 137,
    141, 149
construction 31
Corona, CA 42
cradle to grave 29
Crane, IN 42
CSRS 80, 81, 108, 152
Cuban Missile Crises 57

Dahlgren Laboratory 125
DARPA 21, 38, 53, 152
DDR&E 46, 96, 97, 146
Defense Advanced Projects
    Research Agency. *See*
    DARPA
Defense Agency 40, 52, 54,
    153
Defense Appropriation 140,
    141
Democratic 56
demonstration 20, 22, 27, 28,
    31, 35, 50
Department of Defense.
    See DOD
Department of Energy 57
Department of the Navy. *See*
    DON
Deputy Undersecretary of
    Defense 36
Desert Storm 92, 125
development vi, ix, 12-14,
    19, 21, 22, 24-35, 41, 46, 48,
    50, 51, 60, 61, 65, 84, 107,
    118, 148, 149, 150, 152, 153
Devices 24
Ditch of Death 29, 30
DNL Lab 151

DOD vii, viii, 12-14, 16, 19, 21-23, 26, 28, 30-33, 35-37, 39, 40, 43-49, 52-54, 56, 58-60, 63, 64, 75, 81, 84, 85, 89-92, 96, 98, 111, 112, 118, 131, 140, 145, 146, 148, 149, 150, 151, 152
Dole, Bob 143
DON viii, 57, 145, 147, 149, 150, 151, 152

earmark 37, 86, 87, 129, 135, 136, 137
Economic Stimulus 101
Eisenhower 57, 100, 116
Elected representatives 25
Emperor Hirohito 79
engineering 23, 30, 31, 38, 41, 42, 46, 47, 49, 50, 52, 145, 146, 147, 152
Environmental 23
Erasmus, Desiderius 144
Execution Year 85, 86, 92
Experimental 20

Federal Acquisition 60, 149
Federal agencies 37, 49, 63, 137
Federal Employee Retirement System. *See* FERS
Federal executive ix, 127
Federal Government vi, viii, 11, 15, 58, 61, 62, 74, 79, 132, 141
Federally Funded Research and Development Centers. *See* FFRDC
FERS 80, 81, 108, 152
FFRDC 153
field experiments 27

Financial Management Regulation 22
for-profit 25, 46, 49
Forward Operating Base 97, 98
Foster, Dr. John 146
funding ix, 12, 13, 21, 24-26, 28, 29, 31-33, 35, 36, 38, 40-43, 47, 48, 53, 55, 58, 64, 65, 95, 99-101, 103, 107, 111, 112, 118, 127, 128, 129, 130, 131, 136, 137, 139, 140, 145, 146, 147, 149, 150
FY-13 15, 23, 26, 28, 32, 39, 85, 152
FYDP 27, 31, 32, 152

General 22, 24, 27, 31, 55, 60, 72, 76, 112, 114, 148
George Washington 11
Global Hawk 36
Global Positioning System. *See* GPS
Gorshkov, Admiral Sergey 73
GPS 12, 34, 147, 150
graduate students 23, 29
Great Society 101

HASC 140, 152
high-fidelity 20
Homeland Security 64, 126, 152
Hopper, Grace 120
House and Senate Armed Services Committees. *See* HASC

Independent Research and Development. *See* IR&D
Indian Head, MD 42
Industry 26, 30, 44, 48-50, 52, 55, 58, 60-63, 115, 145, 148, 149, 151
Industry Independent Research and Development. *See* IR&D
Innovation vii, 13, 44, 50, 63, 153
Invention 20, 34
Investment 25, 26, 34, 35, 37, 40, 45-48, 53, 54, 56-58, 60, 61, 63, 113, 131, 136, 149, 151
IR&D 25, 26, 48, 60, 61, 62, 148, 149, 151, 153

Japan 79, 131
Japanese 59, 73, 79, 131
JCTD 98, 153
JFCOM 111, 112, 153
John Lehman 147
Joint Capability Technology Demonstrations. *See* JCTDs
Joint Experimentation Program 111
Joint Forces Command. *See* JFCOM
Joint Requirements Oversight Council. *See* JROC
JROC 40, 152

Lab Director's Fund 55
Laboratory 20, 29-31, 42, 48, 50, 51, 57-59, 61, 124, 125, 146, 147, 150
Laboratory Commander 124
Laboratory studies 20

Laboratory System 43
LFT&E 31
life sciences 23
live fire test and evaluation. *See* LFT&E

Mackie, Walter H. "Tad" x, 100, 121
MANTECH 64
manufacturing 31
Manufacturing Readiness Levels. *See* MRLs
Marine Corps 12, 41, 42, 72, 120, 148, 150, 151, 153
Marine Corps Warfighting Laboratory. *See* MCWL
marketing ix, 127
materiel command 22
mature system 31
McArthur 131, 132
McNamara 22
MCWL 41, 42, 150, 153
MDA 40, 52, 153
Milestone A 23
Milestone B 24, 27, 30, 31
Milestone C 31, 32
military viii, ix, 12-14, 23, 24, 26-28, 31, 37, 38, 41, 42, 48, 53, 54, 57, 60, 66-82, 95, 98, 99, 108, 112, 114, 117, 120, 123, 132, 137, 138, 142, 145, 146, 148
Mohave Desert 51
Montgomery, Hugh vi, vii, ix, 111, 128, 129, 130
MRLs 19, 153

NASA 19, 57
National security 12, 23, 44, 45, 55, 129, 132, 136

Naval ix, 21, 22, 32, 35, 36, 41, 42, 43, 45, 48, 51, 56, 59, 99, 107, 111, 112, 118, 120, 121, 123-125, 128-130, 133, 135, 145-148, 150-154
Naval Air Systems 22, 42
Naval Material Command. *See* NAVMAT
Naval Research Laboratory 41, 51, 59, 83, 150, 153
Naval Sea Systems Command 42
Naval Surface Warfare Center. *See* NSWC
Naval Undersea Warfare Center. *See* NUWC
Naval Warfare Center 42
NAVMAT 145, 146
Navy vi, viii, ix, 12, 22, 26, 35, 36, 41, 42, 48, 51, 53, 56, 57, 59, 71-73, 75, 76, 83, 89-92, 101, 107, 111, 112, 120, 129, 134, 145-148, 150-152
Navy Laboratory and Center Oversight Committee. *See* NLCOC
New Deal 101
Newton, Isaac 108
NLCOC 148, 153
non-profit 25, 47, 52, 56, 62
NSWC 42, 125, 150, 153
NUWC 42, 150, 153

Office of Management and Budget. *See* OMB
Office of Naval Research. *See* ONR
OMB 105, 153
ONR 21, 41, 42, 45, 53, 56, 92, 93, 147, 150, 153

operational systems development 22
operations 20, 31, 36, 120
OPNAV 153

Pacific 59, 126, 131, 132
Pacific Flyway 126
Pakistani 97
Panama City, FL 42
Pareto Optimal 95
Peace Dividend 54, 55, 109, 111
peer-reviewed 24, 45
Penn State 25
Pentagon vii, 13, 73, 74, 96, 99, 112, 117, 122, 136
PL-102-190 60, 149
Policy viii, 12, 32, 43, 49, 55, 67, 70, 74, 79, 82, 107, 111, 115-117, 121, 124, 127, 140, 148
POM 153
Port Hueneme, CA 42
PPBE 153
Predator 36
PRESBUD 13, 37, 38, 45, 47, 57, 141, 153
President's Budget. *See* PRESBUD
Program Element 33, 118, 153
proof of concept 20
proof-of-principle 25
prototype 20, 22, 24, 27, 28, 30, 35, 50, 146
publication 14, 29
public servant vii, 11, 99

Race to the Moon 23, 101
R&D vi, vii, viii, 12-14, 25, 26, 32, 34, 37, 42-47, 55, 59, 61, 63, 66, 73, 84, 131-133, 139, 145-151

RDT&E 13, 19, 21, 22, 23, 30-32, 34, 45, 48, 49, 151, 153
Reagan 26, 44, 48, 52, 57, 111, 149
Recess Appointment 105
Reference A 22, 23, 24, 27, 30, 31, 32
Republican 56
Research and Development. *See* R&D
Research, Development, Test and Evaluation. *See* RDT&E
researcher 23, 29
research grants 24, 49
Resource Sponsor 112, 113, 118, 128, 129, 140
review 21, 24, 29, 31, 32, 40, 48, 60, 71, 77, 129, 138, 148, 149
risk 19, 21, 22, 27-30, 35, 51, 52, 54, 55, 71, 73, 74, 100, 103, 117, 119, 137, 149

SAC 140, 153
SBIR 63, 64, 153
Science and engineering 26
Science and Technology. *See* S&T
scientist 29, 51, 55
SDD 31
SDIO 53, 54, 154
Secretary 34, 44, 107, 111, 121, 129, 130, 145, 147, 148, 152, 153
Secretary of Defense 34, 44, 111, 121
Semper Gumby 74
Senate 105, 121, 140, 153

Senior Executive briefing ix
Senior Executive Service 35, 75, 76, 77, 80, 81, 154
SES 75, 76, 99, 154
SHARP 133
Sheingold, Dr. Leonard 146
Sheingold Report 146
ships 31, 48
simulated environment 20, 27
(Commander) Smith 138
Social Security 81
SONAR 51
Soviet 73
SPAWAR 147, 150, 154
Special Purpose Marine Air-Ground Task Force 42
Sputnik 57
S&T 21, 27, 29, 33, 34, 37, 38, 40-42, 45, 46, 48, 51-54, 56, 58, 59, 61, 63, 102, 111, 112, 118, 120, 121, 124, 125, 128-130, 145, 147, 149-151, 153
Staffer 49
Star Wars 52, 101
STTR 63, 64
studies 20, 24, 31, 61
surveillance 23
Sylvania Electronic Systems 146
Synthetic Hemoglobin Advanced Research Program. *See* SHARP
SYSCOMS 22, 42, 145, 147, 154
system vii, ix, 11-14, 20, 22, 24, 25, 27-33, 35, 36, 41, 42, 46, 50, 52, 56, 57, 62-64, 66-71, 74-81, 84, 94, 95, 99, 110, 113, 122, 123, 127, 130, 142, 143, 147, 150

systematic study 23, 24
system models 27
Systems Command Systems Commander 124
Systems Commands. *See* SYSCOMS

Technical Director 42, 124, 150, 151
technical journal 24, 45
technological progress 23
technologists 29
technology vii, 13, 19-21, 24, 27-29, 32-38, 41, 44, 46, 48, 50-53, 55-57, 63, 64, 102, 118, 120, 146, 152, 153, 154
technology readiness 20
Technology Readiness Level. *See* TRL
The Air Force 41
Thomas Edison 51
Thomas Jefferson 11
Titanic 51
Top Ten List 102, 103
transition vii, 21, 27-30, 35-38, 44, 45, 54, 55, 61, 63, 65, 70, 74-76, 80, 114, 135, 136, 138
TRL vii, 19-22, 24, 26, 28, 36
TRLs vii, 13, 19, 21, 23, 24, 27, 31
Truman, Harry 105

UARC 154
United States 44, 45, 52, 55, 57
university 25, 44, 49, 65, 145, 147
University Affiliated Research Centers. *See* UARC

validation 20

Valley. *See* Valley of Death
Valley of Death 21, 28, 29, 35, 36, 37, 50
VCNO 107, 124
Vice Chief of Naval Operations. *See* VCNO
Viet Nam 26, 45, 58, 147

warfighter 22
Waterman, Dr. Alan 45
weapon 20, 146
Weapon System Elements 32
Weinberger, Caspar 44
White House 105, 109, 123
Woolsey vi, x
Woolsey, R. James vi
World War II (WWII) 51, 52
World War I (WWI) 51

ABOUT THE AUTHOR

Hugh E. Montgomery, Jr.

Hugh E. Montgomery is a Senior Fellow at the Potomac Institute for Policy Studies, following a 35 year career as a Naval scientist and Senior Executive. He served for five years in an Intergovernmental Personnel Act (IPA) assignment as the Executive Director of the Institute for Defense and Homeland Security, and also served as a member of the Defense Science Board Task Force on Energy Strategy. He has focused his efforts on two strategic goals: (1) national energy security; and (2) reinvigoration of the national Science and Technology base and Research and Development infrastructure.

Mr. Montgomery served for 16 years on the staff of the Chief of Naval Operations. As the Department of Navy senior career civilian for Science and Technology requirements and resources, he was Resource Sponsor of a $3 billion R&D account, including all S&T programs executed by the Office of Naval Research. He was the creator of Advanced Technology Demonstrations (ATDs) for technology transition and an architect of the Future Naval Capabilities planning process.

Mr. Montgomery was the first civilian Technical Director of the Marine Corps Warfighting Laboratory and served for four years on the senior staff of the Office of Naval Technology. As the first DON Industry Independent Research and Development (IR&D) Manager, he created and managed the system for oversight and assessment of the multi-billion dollar industry IR&D investment. Earlier senior assignments included Director of Research, Naval Sea Systems Command; Deputy Director, Explosives Division, and Head Technology Branch, Naval Surface Warfare Center. Mr. Montgomery served for 12 years as a Spotsylvania County Planning Commissioner, and is active currently on the Virginia Commission on Energy and Environment and the Virginia Transportation Accountability Commission.

Mr. Montgomery received a BS Degree in Physics and Mathematics from Mississippi College and an MS Degree in Physics from the University of Tennessee. His Physics Ph.D. was completed but not formally awarded, after two dissertation topics each became classified. He also is an International Security Policy graduate of the Kennedy School of Harvard University and an alumnus of the Federal Executive Institute.

Mr. Montgomery lectures frequently on national and international Science and Technology policy, and has published as an authority on R&D, energy and incendiary materials. He was the first person to receive twice the Navy Distinguished Civilian Service Award, the Navy's highest civilian award.

Made in the USA
Middletown, DE
11 September 2024